KEEPING THE DREAM ALIVE

The Cases and Causes of the Southern Poverty Law Center

Southern Poverty Law Center
400 Washington Avenue
Montgomery, Alabama 36104

www.splcenter.org

First published 2014
© 2014 Southern Poverty Law Center

ISBN 978-0-9906990-1-9
Library of Congress Control Number: 2014948724

Designed by Michelle Leland and Russell Estes
Cover photo by Thomas S. England

Published in Montgomery, Alabama, by the Southern Poverty Law Center
Printed in the United States of America

KEEPING THE DREAM ALIVE

The Cases and Causes of the Southern Poverty Law Center

By Booth Gunter

SOUTHERN POVERTY LAW CENTER

Dedicated to those who have the courage to stand up to injustice.

WHEN JOE LEVIN AND I started our work together more than forty years ago, we had some old furniture, one typewriter, and high hopes that we could make a real difference in the lives of the most vulnerable among us.

But not in our wildest dreams did we imagine the Southern Poverty Law Center would accomplish so much and grow into the dynamic organization it is today.

We owe our success to so many people—

Our clients, who have entrusted us with their causes. People like Beulah Mae Donald, who had the courage to take on the Klan in court after her son was lynched.

Our colleagues—too numerous to mention—who have joined us in the Deep South to fight deeply ingrained bigotry and discrimination.

And, especially, our supporters. The truth is, the cases chronicled in this book never would have happened without the moral and financial support of people who share a passion for justice and equality.

This book is dedicated to them—and everyone in our country who has the courage to stand up to injustice.

—MORRIS DEES

GOING AFTER THE KLAN
As the trial approached in the Michael Donald case, Morris Dees and Richard Cohen (third from left) strategized with chief investigator Joe Roy (second from left) and Klanwatch director Bill Stanton (far right). The SPLC's 1987 verdict destroyed the United Klans of America for its role in the lynching of Donald in Mobile, Alabama. Cohen had come to the SPLC as its legal director a year earlier.

FOREWORD

CIVIL RIGHTS BECAME A PASSION for me in 1968. I was only 13, but the events of that year—particularly Dr. King's and Robert Kennedy's assassinations—were hard for even a teen to ignore. I remember watching the Democratic National Convention that summer and being mesmerized by the eloquence of Julian Bond, a young delegate from Georgia who had been one of the founders of the Student Nonviolent Coordinating Committee. Three years later, Julian joined with Morris Dees and Joe Levin to found the Southern Poverty Law Center. He served as our president from 1971 to 1979 and as one of our board members for many years after that. Little could I have imagined while watching Julian on TV as a 13-year-old that, thirty-six years later, I'd become the president of the SPLC and count him, Morris and Joe as my colleagues.

I joined the SPLC as a young lawyer in 1986. The first case I had the privilege of trying with Morris was a criminal contempt action against Glenn Miller and his neo-Nazi organization, then the most dangerous hate group in our country. After the case—we were successful in convicting Miller and his chief lieutenant—Miller's group conspired to bomb our office, and Miller put a white supremacist bounty on Morris' head. The following year, I worked with Morris on our case against the United Klans of America and its members who were responsible for the lynching death of Michael Donald. As many of the readers of this book will know, the United Klans was the hate group that bombed the 16th Street Baptist Church in Birmingham, killing four little girls who were getting dressed for Sunday school. Our case—it was Morris' idea to sue the group for the violence of its members—bankrupted the United Klans and sent the message to others with hate in their hearts that we would move heaven and earth to hold them accountable for the violence they caused.

To be honest, I came to the SPLC thinking that I was a pretty good lawyer. But, practicing alongside Morris, I quickly realized that I had a lot to learn. Never had I seen a lawyer with so much intellect, so much creativity, so much courage, and so much passion for justice. He inspired me then, and he inspires me and everyone at the SPLC today never to rest until, in the words that Dr. King so famously uttered at the great March on Washington, "justice rolls down like waters and righteousness like a mighty stream."

These words are engraved on the Civil Rights Memorial in front of our office. The Memorial, which we built after the Donald case, remembers the martyrs of the movement—people like Dr. King and Medgar Evers and, of course, those four little girls killed in the Birmingham church bombing. The Memorial also chronicles the history of the movement from the Supreme Court's 1954 decision in *Brown v. Board of Education* to Dr. King's assassination in 1968. Between the first entry on the circular Memorial and the last there is a blank space. It symbolizes that the movement didn't begin with the *Brown* decision and didn't end with Dr. King's death. It continues today through the work of people of courage and commitment throughout the country.

My colleagues at the SPLC and I know that the challenges we face today are daunting. We're seeing a resurgence of hate and intolerance in our country and the growing marginalization of those at the bottom of the social and economic ladder. But as the pages of this book reflect, we've met the challenges of the day before. And when we look at the schoolchildren who gather at the Memorial every day and run their hands through the cool waters that ripple across the names of those who gave their lives for justice, we're filled with hope and a sense of obligation to do what we can to keep the dream alive. Standing together, we know we can make a difference.

The march for justice can and must continue.

—J. RICHARD COHEN, PRESIDENT

THE FOUNDING

Morris Dees was managing a thriving publishing business in the late 1960s, one he had been building since his days as an entrepreneurial college student. He was also practicing law—and yearned to take on cases that would help make the promise of the civil rights movement a reality in the Deep South. He sold his business and formed a law partnership with Joe Levin in Montgomery, Alabama. In 1971, Dees and Levin transformed their firm into the nonprofit Southern Poverty Law Center.

BEGINNINGS

MORRIS DEES FACED A DREARY NIGHT.

He needed to be in Chicago for a business meeting, but a snowstorm had stranded him in Cincinnati until morning.

Browsing the airport newsstand, Dees came across the autobiography of one of America's most celebrated lawyers, Clarence Darrow. Reading through the night, he grew more and more captivated by the story of how Darrow had given up a lucrative career as a corporate lawyer to defend union activists and champion the causes of the powerless in a series of high-profile cases.

Dees began to reflect on his own life. At 31, he was managing a highly successful publishing business, a multimillion-dollar enterprise he had been building since his college days at the University of Alabama. He also was practicing law in Montgomery and had begun to take on civil rights cases.

These were momentous times. It was 1968—three years after Dr. Martin Luther King Jr. led thousands of marchers to the white marble steps of the Alabama Capitol to demand an end to American apartheid. It had been the pinnacle of the civil rights movement, a radiant moment that moved the nation to enact important civil rights legislation.

But change was coming slowly to the heart of Dixie. Through the Civil Rights Act of 1964 and the Voting Rights Act of 1965, Congress had forged the legal scaffolding necessary to sweep aside the system of segregation that had been in force for seven decades. White resistance, however, remained strong. Jim Crow wasn't fading away quietly.

As a native son of nearby Mount Meigs, Alabama, Dees had seen plenty of injustice while growing up on his family's small cotton farm. He had witnessed the ravages of segregation up close and personal: the aching poverty; the illiteracy passed down from generation to generation; the lack of hope and the absence of opportunity for advancement; the nonstop degradation and humiliation heaped upon men and women who dared not speak up against it; the unfairness of it all. Despite the time and place, his parents had taught him to respect others, even those whom their society judged inferior by virtue of their race.

For years, Dees had sympathized with the civil rights activists who had challenged the nation's conscience and roiled his city since Rosa Parks refused to give up her bus seat to a white passenger in 1955. He spoke out in favor of desegregation as a student at the University of Alabama after a Klan-inspired mob prevented Autherine Lucy, the school's first black student, from attending classes. After college, he shocked the white congregants at his small, rural church, who walked out when he asked for donations to help rebuild Birmingham's 16th Street Baptist Church after a Klan bomb ripped it open and left four little girls dead. He offended the sensibilities of white Montgomery by holding an integrated Christmas party for his employees at the downtown Jeff Davis Hotel. And he ferried marchers to Selma for the Selma-to-Montgomery voting rights march.

But there was more he could do—much more.

After the long night in Cincinnati with Darrow's story, Dees felt his priorities shifting. "I was ready to take that step," he later wrote. "Little had changed in the South. Whites held the power and had no intention of voluntarily sharing it. Blacks were excluded from good jobs, decent housing, elective office, good educations, jury service, and a host of other aspects of the community enjoyed by whites."

By the time his plane landed in Chicago, he had decided to sell his thriving company and devote his time to civil rights. "All the things in my life that had brought me to this point, all the pulls and tugs of my conscience, found a singular peace. It did not matter what my neighbors would think, or the judges, the bankers, or even my relatives."

BY DECEMBER OF 1969, Dees had sold his business and filed several more civil rights lawsuits.

Earlier that year, two African-American cousins, both just 7, had wanted to attend the YMCA's summer camp at nearby Lake Jordan. But the organization said no black children were allowed.

The boys, Vincent and Edward Smith, became Dees' clients. And over the next few years, Dees became, as *Time* magazine later called him, the "second most hated man in Alabama." (The first was famed U.S. District Judge Frank M. Johnson Jr., before whom Dees would often practice.)

The case was not a simple one. Dees knew that federal civil rights laws had not been interpreted to prohibit private organizations like the YMCA from discriminating. No court had previously ordered a private group to integrate unless there was proof of substantial government involvement. The YMCA, meanwhile, was backed by Montgomery's most powerful people—white elites who fiercely opposed the idea of white and black children playing together. But Dees found a smoking gun hidden deep within the boxes of documents he subpoenaed. In 1958, the city had faced a lawsuit seeking to integrate its

"whites-only" recreational facilities, a network of parks with swimming pools, tennis courts and other amenities. Rather than chance a court ruling, city leaders had simply closed the parks and filled the swimming pools with dirt. In secret, they drafted an agreement with the YMCA to continue providing recreational activities on a segregated basis. Further, the city and the YMCA established a joint "coordinating committee" to oversee the new arrangement. The impact was extraordinary. In the time since the agreement, the YMCA had grown from a thousand to eighteen thousand members and had added numerous branches and swimming pools—all segregated.

Armed with this information, Dees won the case. "The YMCA merely exchanged places with the city as provider of recreation for the neighborhood," wrote Judge Johnson. A federal appellate court agreed, the Smith cousins were admitted to summer camp, and the YMCA was forced to open its facilities to everyone. Another barrier to equality had been shattered.

Dees, meanwhile, was becoming an outcast in his own community. He had faced hostility before because of his liberal positions. After the Selma-to-Montgomery march, a sheriff's deputy had showed up at Dees' mother's house with a warning: "Bubba [Dees' nickname] should be careful associating with those communists and niggers or his reputation will be ruined." A cross had been burned in front of his publishing business, and his home was broken into on the same night. Later, someone vandalized his office, carving KKK into its plaster walls. But, as he threw himself into the practice of law full time, the pressure increased, and he and his wife were ostracized by their former friends and neighbors. His two young sons were no longer invited to birthday parties, and theirs were sparsely attended. Other parents stopped waving back at ball games. Threatening phone calls became common. In later years, the threats would become more serious.

CONTINUED ON **PAGE 18**

LESSONS LEARNED IN CHILDHOOD

Morris Dees, here at age 16, grew up working alongside African-American field hands in the dusty cotton fields of his father's small farm in Mount Meigs, Alabama. He saw firsthand the deprivations and rank injustices faced by black people during the Jim Crow era. Later, as a student at the University of Alabama in the 1950s, he spoke out in favor of desegregation after a Klan-inspired mob prevented Autherine Lucy, the school's first black student, from attending classes.

THE FIRST TIME IN COURT TOGETHER, 1969

In their first case together, Morris Dees and Joe Levin represented Mac McCarley (middle), an Alabama state senator who was accused of corruption. The two lawyers won an acquittal in the high-profile criminal case, which became the Associated Press' news story of the year in Alabama. But, more important, they discovered they worked well together and soon formed the legal partnership that would, two years later, become the Southern Poverty Law Center.

JOE LEVIN'S AWAKENING TO HATE

By his own account, Levin enjoyed the party atmosphere during his time at the University of Alabama, where he lived in this Jewish fraternity house, and was largely oblivious to what was happening in the civil rights movement. But in 1962, Klansmen burned a cross on the lawn after a fraternity brother published an editorial calling for the University of Mississippi to admit a black student. Levin began to re-examine his belief system and could no longer ignore others who were targeted because of racism: "What I had learned all my life was wrong."

THE YEAR DEES SUED THE YMCA, Joe Levin returned to his hometown of Montgomery to begin a career in his father's commercial law practice. Like Dees, he had studied law at the University of Alabama. Now, after serving two years in the Army, he had come home to launch his legal career.

Levin had been in junior high school in 1955, the year Rosa Parks' act of civil disobedience sparked the Montgomery bus boycott. Like many whites, he was largely oblivious to the tectonic shifts shaking the earth around him. That changed during his time in college.

In 1962, one of Levin's fraternity brothers, Melvin Meyer, was editor of the campus newspaper, *The Crimson White*, and published an editorial calling for the University of Mississippi to admit James Meredith, a black student. Levin's school was the same university where, the next year, segregationist Governor George Wallace would mount his symbolic—and fruitless—"stand in the schoolhouse door" to prevent African-American students from enrolling. Levin's courageous fraternity brother was harassed and threatened by his fellow students, and early one morning, members of the United Klans of America burned a cross on the lawn of Levin's Jewish fraternity house.

At first, Levin was angry that the actions of his fraternity brother had disrupted his "routine of drinking and going to football games." But the burning cross was a wake-up call. Levin began to re-examine his entire belief system. "Prior to that time, I saw myself as a white Southerner," he later recalled. "I had not experienced that kind of naked hatred. Once my eyes were opened, I couldn't ignore others who were persecuted around me. What I had learned all my life was wrong."

During his first year back in Montgomery, Levin followed the YMCA case closely in the newspaper and admired Dees' work in other civil rights cases.

He mentioned to Dees' brother, whom he had known in college, that he would like to help. It wasn't long before Dees asked Levin to assist in the defense of a state legislator accused of corruption. The case didn't involve civil rights, but it was the beginning of a historic partnership.

Dees and Levin won that case. What's more, they found they worked well together. Dees later wrote that in Levin he "recognized a natural born trial lawyer."

Both men yearned to take on cases that mattered, cases that would advance the cause of social justice and help cast into stone the changes for which Dr. King and others had sacrificed so much. They soon started a law firm and agreed they would charge the clients who could afford to pay but work free for those who couldn't.

THE LAW FIRM LEVIN & DEES found immediate success. Early on, the two lawyers won a large fee in a case in which a white developer had taken advantage of a black woman. With that, they were able to finance a number of civil rights cases. They represented a high school English teacher who was fired for teaching a Kurt Vonnegut short story. They sued the local newspaper, the *Montgomery Advertiser*, over its discriminatory practice of printing wedding announcements for black couples on the Thursday "Negro news" page rather than on the Sunday society page, where announcements for white couples were featured. They brought suit to change the electoral system that kept African Americans out of the Alabama Legislature. And, in a groundbreaking gender-discrimination case that would reach the U.S. Supreme Court, they successfully sued the U.S. Department of Defense for denying servicewomen the same benefits to which men were entitled.

It wasn't long before both men knew they had

CONTINUED ON **PAGE 23**

THE BIRMINGHAM CHURCH BOMBING
On Sept. 15, 1963, four Klansmen committed one of the most heinous terrorist acts of the civil rights movement, planting a bomb at the 16th Street Baptist Church in Birmingham. The church had been used as an organizing hub for civil rights demonstrators and a training site for those who took part in the Children's Crusade to demand the integration of the city's public accommodations. The bomb, made of dynamite with a timing device, blasted a hole in the church's rear wall. Four girls were killed as they prepared with other children for the Sunday morning service. Killed were (from top): Cynthia Wesley, 14; Addie Mae Collins, 14; Denise McNair, 11; and Carole Robertson, 14. Twenty-two other people were injured. Though one Klansman was identified early on, he wasn't convicted until seventeen years later, after Alabama Attorney General Bill Baxley reopened the case in 1971. Two others were later convicted; the other had already died.

THE SELMA-TO-MONTGOMERY VOTING RIGHTS MARCH

Some twenty-five thousand voting rights marchers led by Dr. Martin Luther King Jr. reached the Alabama Capitol in Montgomery on March 25, 1965. They hoped to deliver a petition to Governor George Wallace but were blocked by a line of state troopers. The Dexter Avenue Baptist Church, where King preached during the Montgomery bus boycott, can be seen on the left (center). In a thunderous address to the marchers, King invoked the names of those who had died during the struggle for equality—including the four girls killed in the Birmingham church bombing: "[W]e must go on and be sure that they did not die in vain. The pattern of their feet as they walked through Jim Crow barriers in the great stride toward freedom is the thunder of the marching men of Joshua, and the world rocks beneath their tread." The nation was moved, and a little more than four months later Congress passed the Voting Rights Act of 1965.

THE YMCA DISCRIMINATION CASE

In 1969, Morris Dees took a case on behalf of two 7-year-old African-American cousins in Montgomery who wanted to attend the YMCA's summer camp at a nearby lake. The organization, which operated segregated swimming pools and other facilities across the city, claimed it was a private organization and no black children were allowed. But Dees uncovered documents showing a secret arrangement with city officials whereby the YMCA would provide segregated recreational facilities on behalf of the city in an effort to avoid integrating city pools, which were filled with dirt to keep black children from using them. Dees won the case, successfully integrating the YMCA, but soon started receiving threats from the Ku Klux Klan.

found their calling. They wanted to dedicate their careers to helping the powerless and the forgotten, those who were falling through the cracks in society. They wanted to take on tough cases that could make a difference in the lives of people across the South and the rest of the country who were facing discrimination and injustice.

But to represent clients who couldn't pay, they needed continuing financial support. So, in 1971, they established a nonprofit organization and called it the Southern Poverty Law Center, a name that reflected their location and the fact that their cases were intended to target customs, practices and laws that were used to keep African Americans—and also low-income whites—powerless.

Julian Bond agreed to become the organization's first president. Though he was just 31, Bond was a nationally known civil rights leader and a founder of the Student Nonviolent Coordinating Committee in the early 1960s. He had won a seat in the Georgia Legislature in 1965, but lawmakers there had refused to seat him because of his opposition to the Vietnam War. He sued and eventually won the case in the U.S. Supreme Court. Dees and Levin also recruited an advisory council composed of civil rights stalwarts, including John Lewis, an Alabama native who was bloodied in the Selma-to-Montgomery march and who would later be elected to Congress from Georgia.

When it came to seeking support for the new nonprofit, Dees had an idea. Using a list of names obtained from other progressive groups, he mailed out twenty-five thousand letters seeking support for the defense of an indigent black man who was facing the death penalty after being indicted on circumstantial evidence by an all-white grand jury. More than five hundred people responded with donations to support the case and the SPLC's other work.

At the same time, Dees was active on the national political scene, serving as the chief fundraiser for the presidential campaign of South Dakota Senator George McGovern. Though McGovern was defeated by President Richard M. Nixon in 1972, Dees' small-donor, direct-mail techniques revolutionized campaign fundraising and raised a record amount of money through the mail. When the campaign was over, McGovern gave Dees the list of his nearly seven hundred thousand supporters to kick-start his fledgling organization. More than one hundred thousand of those people eventually became members of the SPLC, helping establish a sound financial base that would power the organization for years to come.

Dees and Levin hired a small staff, and from then on, the SPLC never charged another client for its services. Over the next four decades, the organization litigated cases that stamped out remnants of Jim Crow segregation, put violent factions of the Ku Klux Klan and other white supremacist groups out of business, and protected the rights of children, women, the disabled, migrant workers, LGBT people and others who faced discrimination and exploitation.

As it grew in size and stature, the SPLC blazed new paths. To fight prejudice, the organization introduced a program called Teaching Tolerance to create anti-bias films (including two that won Oscars), books, and other materials for America's classrooms, and distribute them, free of charge, to teachers across the country. And it launched what is today an internationally known investigative unit that tracks and exposes the activities of hate groups to the public, the media and law enforcement agencies nationwide.

This, in the following pages, is the remarkable story of the cases and causes of the Southern Poverty Law Center, the organization started by two Alabama lawyers who wanted to make a difference, supported by hundreds of thousands of Americans who share their commitment to justice and equality. •

SELLING COOKBOOKS

By the mid-1960s, Morris Dees' business was the leading cookbook publisher in the country, selling more than three million volumes each year. But he and his business partner, Millard Fuller, were both destined for the nonprofit world. Fuller left the company to start what would later become Habitat for Humanity. In 1967, Dees was named one of the Jaycees' ten "Outstanding Young Men in America." Another was a young consumer rights lawyer who was stirring up the business and political establishment in Washington: Ralph Nader. The next year, Dees sold the business to concentrate on his fledgling civil rights work in the courts.

REBUILDING AFTER ARSON

Morris Dees and Joe Levin break ground for a new SPLC office building in May 1984. The construction followed the 1983 firebombing of the SPLC's first office by Alabama Klansmen. The new building, situated less than a block from the church where Dr. Martin Luther King Jr. preached during the civil rights movement, was transformed into the Civil Rights Memorial Center in 2005.

REPRESENTING THE VULNERABLE
Morris Dees talks with an inmate at Holman Prison in Atmore, Alabama, in 1972. Throughout its history, the SPLC has represented the most vulnerable and disadvantaged members of society, including death row inmates and other prisoners.

JULIAN BOND, FIRST SPLC PRESIDENT
Civil rights leader Julian Bond speaks as a Georgia delegate at the Democratic National Convention in Chicago on Aug. 28, 1968, just months after the assassinations of Dr. Martin Luther King Jr. and Robert F. Kennedy. Three years later, Bond became the first president of the SPLC, serving until 1979. He later served on the organization's board of directors for many years. Bond also helped found the Student Nonviolent Coordinating Committee in the early 1960s and later became chairman of the NAACP.

CAMPAIGNING FOR McGOVERN

Morris Dees catches a private moment with U.S. Senator George McGovern aboard a plane during the 1972 presidential campaign. As McGovern's chief fundraiser, Dees raised a record amount of money through the mail and revolutionized campaign fundraising with his small-donor, direct-mail techniques. More than one hundred thousand of McGovern's supporters eventually became members of the SPLC, helping to establish a sound financial base for the organization in its early years. The longtime South Dakota senator remained a close friend of Dees and the SPLC until his death in 2012.

THE 1976 PRESIDENTIAL RACE

Morris Dees served as finance director for Jimmy Carter's presidential campaign in 1976, spending six months in Atlanta while Joe Levin ran the SPLC office. Following the campaign, Dees was offered a position in the new administration but decided to return to Montgomery. He was invited frequently to White House events, and spent a Rose Garden lunch lobbying the president to end the death penalty. Carter appointed Levin to head his transition team for the U.S. Justice Department and then as chief counsel at the National Highway Traffic Safety Administration, the agency that regulates automobile and truck safety. During Levin's tenure, NHTSA issued the nation's first fuel-efficiency standards for vehicles and the first rules requiring all cars to have either air bags or automatic seat belts.

ON SUNDAY, SEPTEMBER 22, 1963, I bowed my head in my small Baptist church and offered a prayer for the four little black girls who had been killed by a Klansman's bomb the previous Sunday in their Baptist church in Birmingham.

When I looked up, my wife and I were standing alone. Everyone else in our all-white congregation had walked out.

Little could I have imagined then that one day I'd file a lawsuit that would bankrupt the very Klan group that was responsible for that church bombing. And little could I have realized then that thousands of people around the country would be standing with me and my colleagues at the Southern Poverty Law Center as we pursue justice for those who have no other champion and teach acceptance and understanding to millions of young people across the nation.

As I look at the Civil Rights Memorial in front of our office today, I think about those four little girls and about the other martyrs of the movement whose names are inscribed in the Memorial's black granite. And as I contemplate the words of Dr. King—"we will not be satisfied until justice rolls down like waters"—I renew my vow to continue our fight for as long as it takes to rid this nation of injustice.

Neither the Klan's firebombing of our office nor the many serious death threats we've received over the years have dampened my resolve.

Our success owes as much to the thousands of passionate people who have pledged their moral and financial support to our cause as it does to me or the dedicated men and women who work with me every day.

—MORRIS DEES

CHAPTER ONE

BURYING JIM CROW

FEW INSTITUTIONS SYMBOLIZED the brutality and systematic oppression faced by African Americans in the Deep South more than the all-white ranks of the Alabama State Troopers.

In 1963, helmeted troopers flanked Governor George Wallace during his symbolic "stand in the schoolhouse door" at the University of Alabama, where the segregationist governor attempted to block the enrollment of two black students. Two years later, a trooper killed civil rights activist Jimmie Lee Jackson during a brawl initiated by troopers swinging billy clubs during a march in Marion, Alabama. Then, on a pivotal day now known as "Bloody Sunday," troopers tear-gassed and clubbed peaceful civil rights marchers on the Edmund Pettus Bridge in Selma.

By 1972, despite the success of the civil rights movement, Alabama's trooper force remained a bastion of segregation; there had not been a single black trooper in its thirty-seven-year history. That year, the Southern Poverty Law Center filed suit on behalf of Phillip Paradise, an African-American man who had been denied the right to apply for a job as a trooper.

Paradise v. Allen was among a series of important cases brought by the SPLC in the early 1970s as it embarked on a legal campaign to stamp out vestiges of Jim Crow. Congress had enacted new civil rights laws, but that didn't mean the white establishment in Alabama and other Deep South states would comply voluntarily. It would take lawyers like Morris Dees and Joe Levin to fight the battles, one by one, in court.

The trooper case landed in the court of U.S. District Judge Frank M. Johnson Jr., who had earlier heard Dees' case challenging the Montgomery YMCA's discriminatory admission policies. In the trooper case, Johnson found "a blatant and continuous pattern and practice of discrimination" in violation of the 14th Amendment. He ordered the Alabama Department of Public Safety, which oversaw the state's highway patrol, to hire one black trooper for every white until African Americans made up 25 percent of the force.

State officials resisted, however, and imposed a virtual ban on hiring in the mid-1970s. The number of troopers steadily declined through attrition, and those African Americans hired before the freeze found little opportunity to advance through the ranks. After repeated efforts to enforce the ruling by SPLC lawyers, the case finally reached the U.S. Supreme Court. In 1987, Dees asked Richard Cohen, a 31-year-old lawyer who had arrived at the SPLC only two months earlier, to handle the oral argument. Cohen, who came from a law firm in Washington, D.C., had tried cases in court but never handled appellate work. He didn't hesitate, telling Dees, "Of course I'm up for it."

In this case, Cohen was going up against the Reagan administration's Justice Department, which had asked the Court to reverse the lower court's order.

In a landmark 1987 decision, the Court upheld the race-based promotion plan previously won by the SPLC.

Still, the litigation dragged on until 1995—twenty-three years after it began. The final outcome was not only a victory for racial equality but a testament to the tenacity and staying power of the SPLC.

Phillip Paradise never joined the trooper force, instead becoming a firefighter. But one of the beneficiaries of the case was a woman named Glenda Deese. In 1980, she became the state's first black female trooper cadet. "I just focused on working hard and being the best I could be," she said. "All I needed was an opportunity to prove myself." And she did, rising to be the second-highest-ranking official in the Alabama Department of Public Safety during a twenty-six-year law enforcement career.

Deese was not alone. By the turn of the century, the trooper force was transformed from a symbol of oppression into an affirmative action success story, with the highest percentage of minority officers in the nation. In 2011, a former SPLC client, Hugh McCall, became the director of the Alabama Department of Public Safety—the first black officer to lead the troopers.

AT THE SAME TIME the SPLC was litigating the trooper case in the early 1970s, it was pursuing other lawsuits that would shatter racial barriers and change the legal landscape.

Representing civil rights activist E.D. Nixon, the architect of the Montgomery bus boycott, the SPLC challenged a state election system that diluted the voting power of Alabama's African Americans so much that in 1970 there were just two black legislators. In fact, even though black people made up 25 percent of the state's population, the two legislators were the only African Americans elected to the Legislature since the Jim Crow system of apartheid took effect nearly a century earlier.

CONTINUED ON **PAGE 40**

INTEGRATING THE ALABAMA STATE TROOPERS
When the SPLC sued the Alabama Highway Patrol on behalf of Phillip Paradise (above) in 1972, there had never been a black trooper in the state. The SPLC suit forced the state to integrate its trooper force. At right, African-American troopers receive their certification in 1973 following a settlement. The initial victory would prove short-lived, however, as the state resisted promoting black troopers and eventually instituted a hiring freeze to circumvent the mandate.

THE TROOPER CASE—FINAL ARGUMENT

Richard Cohen (right) spoke to reporters outside of the U.S. Supreme Court in 1987 after arguing the final appeal in the case that integrated the Alabama state trooper force. In a landmark decision, the Court upheld a race-based promotion plan previously won by the SPLC—over the objections of the Reagan administration's Justice Department. Cohen, who came to the SPLC as its legal director the previous year, became president of the organization in 2003 and continues to lead it today. Glenda Deese (above) became the state's first black female trooper cadet in 1980, even as the court battle raged. She rose to be the state's second-highest-ranking official in the Alabama Department of Public Safety and later became the SPLC's deputy security director. By the turn of the century, Alabama's trooper force had become a model for the rest of the country, with the highest percentage of minority officers.

TAKING DOWN THE CONFEDERATE FLAG

The Confederate battle flag was raised over the Alabama Capitol by Governor George Wallace in 1963 after he was elected on a segregationist platform. It remained there for thirty years. The flag, a symbol of racism and oppression, was used to antagonize voting rights marchers during the Selma-to-Montgomery march in 1965. The SPLC in 1992 sued the state on behalf of an African-American legislator, pointing to an obscure 1891 statute that said only the state and national flags could be flown over the Capitol dome. A judge agreed, and the flag was removed.

This was another instance in which Congress, through the Voting Rights Act, had paved the way for black citizens to achieve equality but legal action was required to make that promise a reality. The SPLC aimed to dismantle Alabama's at-large voting system, which submerged areas with large black populations into multimember legislative districts dominated by white majorities.

In 1972, a federal court decided in favor of Nixon and the SPLC, and the Supreme Court affirmed the ruling. To ensure that black voters would have an equal opportunity to elect representatives of their choice, the court required the Legislature to reapportion itself into districts each represented by a single member so that African Americans couldn't be gerrymandered into large districts with multiple at-large representatives.

The legal effort paid off immediately. Fifteen African Americans were elected to the Alabama Legislature during the election in 1974, the first held after the court ruling.

THOUGH THE SPLC STAFF WAS SMALL in the 1970s, its footprint was large.

Dozens of lawsuits were filed to champion the rights of African Americans and impoverished whites. In one case, the SPLC represented a black orphan who had been sent to a detention center for juvenile delinquents at age 10 because, except for one small group home, state-licensed shelters wouldn't take black children. In Alabama and other states, the SPLC challenged discriminatory hiring practices in municipal governments and federal agencies; the lack of due process in foreclosure proceedings used by banks to take the homes of the poor; the use of public facilities by all-white "segregation" academies; the expulsion from school of pregnant teens; government policies that resulted in racially segregated public housing; the use of mentally disabled children in medical experiments; state policies that denied federal welfare benefits to those in need; and much more. Not all cases were won, but more often than not they led to reform, because even when a favorable court decision was not rendered, the injustices exposed by the SPLC could not withstand the light of day.

One such case involved the forced sterilization of young African-American girls. The Relf sisters—Minnie Lee, 14, and Mary Alice, 12—lived in public housing in Montgomery. In 1973, welfare workers picked up the girls and their mother and took them to a local doctor. The mother, who couldn't read or write, was told the girls would be given routine shots, so she placed an "X" on a form to denote her approval. The sisters were then transported to a hospital funded and controlled by the federal Office of Economic Opportunity, an agency established in 1964 to administer anti-poverty programs. The next morning, doctors performed tubal ligations on both girls. Unbeknownst to the mother, several years earlier, an older sister had been repeatedly given unsolicited injections of an experimental birth control drug. A few days after the sterilizations of Minnie Lee and Mary Alice, welfare workers came for the older sister, who hid in a closet and refused to go.

The SPLC sued the federal government on behalf of the Relf sisters in 1973, charging that government agencies had violated their constitutional rights to due process and equal protection. The agencies had, according to the complaint, "sought out the Relf

children as good experimental subjects for their family planning program." A federal judge, finding that countless women had been forced to undergo sterilization under threat of losing welfare benefits, prohibited the use of federal funds for this purpose. As the litigation moved through the courts, the government withdrew the regulations under which these sterilizations were conducted and required that doctors obtain "informed consent" before performing them.

Many of the SPLC's cases brought relief to African Americans who had long suffered under Jim Crow only to see change come slowly after the civil rights movement. In 1971, for example, the SPLC sued to rectify a twenty-year injustice on behalf of a neighborhood association that represented the African-American residents of a small, unincorporated community near Selma, Alabama. A federal court responded by ordering the paving of 10 miles of streets that had been neglected by local officials. The case not only made a tangible difference in the lives of the SPLC's clients, it put other Southern communities on notice that they could be held accountable for discriminating against black residents in providing such basic services.

SPLC lawyers not only targeted government policies but, on occasion, cultural customs as well. In 1973, the SPLC went to court to fight for a black man named Wilbur Oliver of Mansura, Louisiana. Two years earlier, Oliver had contacted a local, white-owned funeral home to arrange for the burial of his mother. The Escude Funeral Home agreed to embalm the woman but, because she was black, refused to allow her wake to be held on its premises—even though the woman, the community's midwife, had delivered and nursed some of the Escude children. The only other funeral home in town would not handle black bodies at all. When Oliver could find no local attorney to challenge the practice, his priest contacted the SPLC.

Within a month after the SPLC filed a class action suit, a federal court declared that the funeral home's actions were illegal.

Oliver, who had lost his left arm to a Spanish moss-cleaning machine early in life, was a laborer who earned a meager living cutting sugar cane and raising vegetables. His priest, Father August Thompson, characterized him as "one of the common people and not a crusader."

"[I]t is usually the ordinary people who make a difference by doing extraordinary things," Father Thompson said. "We never know what we're capable of doing until we do it."

The Oliver ruling reverberated far beyond the town of sixteen hundred people. It established a precedent that funeral homes everywhere had to provide equal services, at the same prices, to all people.

And it was one more nail in Jim Crow's coffin.

ANOTHER SYSTEMIC INJUSTICE that was rooted in the Jim Crow policies of the Deep South was the application of the death penalty. African Americans accused of murder, especially those accused of killing a white person, were far more likely to die in the state's electric chair than were white defendants. It was an area ripe for intervention by the SPLC.

In the 1970s, Alabama's death penalty law had a peculiar feature. In a capital murder trial, a jury had only two choices: convict and sentence the defendant to death, or acquit. Juries were not allowed to find the defendant guilty of a lesser offense. That's how Gilbert Beck found himself on death row.

Beck, who was white, was arrested in 1977 after he and an accomplice robbed an 80-year-old man in his home. There was no question that Beck participated in the robbery and that he deserved to be punished; he admitted his guilt at trial. But he didn't kill the victim. He had been about to tie him up when

Morris Dees meets with the Relfs, an impoverished family living in public housing in Montgomery, Alabama. In 1973, doctors working with a federal welfare agency performed surgeries to sterilize two girls—Minnie Lee, 14, and Mary Alice, 12—without the family's consent or prior knowledge. After the SPLC sued on their behalf, the government stopped the program. "I was mad. I wouldn't have let them do that," the girls' mother, Minnie, told a Senate committee chaired by Edward Kennedy. A federal judge found that under federally funded programs countless women had been coerced to undergo sterilization under threat of losing welfare benefits. In addition, numerous states since the 1920s had enacted eugenics laws that led to the compulsory sterilization of some sixty-five thousand people.

THE TARBORO THREE
Three innocent black men, known as the Tarboro Three, were sentenced to die in North Carolina's gas chamber for the rape of a white woman in 1973. After spending two years behind bars, the men (from left: Vernon Leroy Brown, Bobby Hines and Jesse Lee Walston) were granted a new trial after SPLC lawyers uncovered key evidence that had not been introduced at their trial. Prosecutors then agreed to release the men if they pleaded "no contest" to reduced charges. They were set free in 1975.

his accomplice unexpectedly struck the man and killed him.

Under Alabama's statute, jurors were told that unless they convicted Beck of the capital crime of intentionally killing the victim in the course of a robbery, he would go free and he could never be tried again for what he had done. Jurors were not even allowed to consider the lesser crimes of first-degree murder or manslaughter or to recommend a sentence other than death.

So, predictably, the jury convicted Beck and sentenced him to die in Alabama's electric chair.

Alabama's death penalty statute was the only one of its kind in the country. Then-Governor George Wallace had signed it into law in 1975, saying, "I hope we'll see some electrocutions in this state." Later in the decade, a successful state attorney general candidate was reported as saying, "I'll fry [violent criminals] until their eyeballs pop out and smoke comes out their ears."

Believing Beck's conviction was an injustice and that Alabama's statute was inherently unfair, the SPLC took up the inmate's appeal.

And on June 20, 1980, the U.S. Supreme Court agreed, ruling 7-2 that the statute violated the Constitution. The convictions of Beck and ten other

inmates awaiting execution in Alabama were vacated, and new trials were ordered. "For death row inmates in Alabama, this was an incredibly important decision," said John Carroll, who served as SPLC legal director at the time and handled the case.

The Supreme Court said the law created the risk that a jury would convict a defendant of capital murder simply to avoid letting him go free when there was evidence of a violent crime. "[T]he failure to give the jury the 'third option' of convicting on a lesser included offense would seem inevitably to enhance the risk of an unwarranted conviction," wrote Justice John Paul Stevens. "Such a risk cannot be tolerated in a case in which the defendant's life is at stake."

Beck v. Alabama was just one of the cases the SPLC pursued in the 1970s as it sought justice for those unfairly sentenced to die.

In another high-profile death penalty case, the SPLC succeeded in freeing three innocent young black men—known as the Tarboro Three—who were sentenced to die in North Carolina's gas chamber for the rape of a white woman in 1973. The men spent two years behind bars before the SPLC won a new trial after uncovering key evidence that had not been presented at the original trial. Rather than retry them, prosecutors agreed to release the men from prison if they pleaded "no contest" to reduced charges. They accepted the offer, even though they earlier had refused to plead guilty to rape charges in exchange for a lighter sentence, saying they could not admit to a crime they didn't commit.

In another case, Johnny Ross, 16, became the nation's youngest death row inmate in 1975 when he was convicted of raping a white woman in Louisiana. Ross, an African American, was arrested more than a week after the rape even though he didn't match the woman's description of the assailant and she could not identify him in a lineup. Ross said he was beaten until he signed a confession. SPLC lawyers who appealed his case proved his innocence using blood tests that should have been introduced in the original trial.

Not only did SPLC lawyers take on such cases, they used trials as laboratories to perfect various techniques. Then, as the organization shifted its attention to other areas of the law, it shared the lessons in seminars and manuals to guide other defense lawyers across the country.

EVEN DECADES AFTER the civil rights movement, African Americans in many Deep South communities stood little chance of receiving justice in the courts when victimized by whites.

Such was the case for Billy Ray Johnson.

Johnson, a 42-year-old black man with mental disabilities, lived in the tiny East Texas town of Linden. Shortly after midnight on September 28, 2003, he was waiting for a ride at a convenience store when a young white man asked if he wanted to join about fifteen others at a party in his father's cow pasture. Johnson, childlike and trusting, was acquainted with the 19-year-old man and got into the car with him. He soon found himself drinking beer and dancing around a campfire. It wasn't long before laughter turned to jeers as some of the partiers, all of whom were white and in their late teens or early twenties, began to tease and taunt Johnson. Someone called him a "crazy nigger." Someone asked why the "stupid nigger" had been brought to the party.

CONTINUED ON **PAGE 52**

YOUNGEST DEATH ROW INMATE
In 1975, 16-year-old Johnny Ross was convicted of raping a white woman in Louisiana, becoming the youngest person on death row. Ross did not match the description of the rapist, and the victim could not identify him in a lineup. But he had signed a confession, he said, after being beaten by lawmen. The SPLC took up his case on appeal and proved his innocence with blood tests that weren't used in the original trial. In 2005, the Supreme Court outlawed the death penalty for crimes committed by defendants under the age of 18.

THE ROY PATTERSON CASE

Twenty-five-old Roy Patterson was a U.S. Marine who served in Vietnam and was stationed in Georgia, where he lived with his wife and newborn son. One night in 1975, when he stopped at an out-of-the-way gas station with family members in the town of Cordele, his brother was arrested and taken to jail without any apparent cause. When Patterson arrived at the police station, he and his family were threatened and assaulted by a white state trooper, who pulled out his gun. As he tried to defend his family from the trooper, who had a history of violence against African Americans, two officers were killed. Patterson was convicted of capital murder amid an ugly racist atmosphere and sentenced to life in prison. After a series of appeals, the SPLC won his release in 1988.

THE EARL CHARLES CASE
Earl Charles (fourth from left), who spent more than three years on death row for two murders he didn't commit, with Morris Dees, SPLC lawyer Dennis Balske (second from left) and family members outside of a Savannah, Georgia, courthouse in 1980. An SPLC lawsuit accused a police detective of encouraging witnesses to wrongfully identify Charles and of covering up proof that he was in another city when the murders were committed. The SPLC won a $75,000 settlement from the city.

JUSTICE FOR LOYAL GARNER JR.

Loyal Garner Jr., a 34-year-old truck driver from Louisiana, was arrested on a traffic charge in the East Texas town of Hemphill on Christmas Day 1987. While locked up in the Sabine County Jail, he was dragged from his cell and brutally beaten by the police chief and sheriff's deputies. Left without medical treatment, he died two days later. To seek justice for Garner's widow and six children, the SPLC brought suit and reached a settlement with the town. SPLC lawyers also uncovered evidence that led state prosecutors to file criminal charges against the men who killed Garner; all three were convicted and sent to prison.

THE JOANNE LITTLE CASE

Joanne Little was awaiting a hearing in the Beaufort County Jail in North Carolina in August 1974 when a jailer with an ice pick came into her cell and attempted to rape her. She fought back and stabbed him, then fled the jail as he lay dying. She later turned herself in and was charged with capital murder. With its racial and sexual overtones, the case drew wide public attention, leading to demonstrations and petitions in support of Little from feminist and minority groups. With the SPLC underwriting the defense and providing legal support, she was acquitted in 1975.

By 2 a.m., only four young men, a woman and Johnson remained. One suggested hitting Johnson, and another told him to "leave before the KKK comes and gets you." When Johnson said he wanted to finish his beer first, it was knocked out of his hand. Then one of the men, who had been a baseball pitcher in high school, punched him hard in the face. Johnson fell backward and hit his head. Unconscious, he vomited and began to make a gurgling noise.

A hospital was only a mile away. But no one took him. Instead, they stood over Johnson for an hour, debating what to do. One of the men worried about losing his job as a jailer. Finally, they tossed Johnson's limp body in the back of a pickup truck and drove away. They dumped him, still unconscious, beside a dark, deserted road, where he landed in a fire ant bed. Then they went to a car wash to clean the blood and vomit from the truck bed.

Johnson was found the next day after one of the men called the sheriff's office to report seeing "a man passed out on the ground." He was alive but had suffered a brain hemorrhage that left him with severe, permanent brain damage affecting his ability to speak, talk or take care of himself. After three weeks in the hospital, he spent another three weeks in rehabilitation before being transferred to a nursing home to spend, most likely, the rest of his life.

Though they concocted a story of self-defense in the event their roles in the crime were discovered, things quickly unraveled for the four men who had been at the scene after they were arrested. But the criminal justice system in Linden, situated in a region long plagued by virulent racism, would offer little in the way of justice for Johnson. Predominantly white juries rejected felony charges, convicting the men instead on lesser misdemeanor charges and recommended no jail time. A judge, who had no choice under Texas law, sentenced three of the men to thirty days in jail, and the fourth to sixty—barely slaps on the wrist.

Johnson's family was outraged. "I didn't go to law school, and I'm not an educated man," Lue Wilson, Johnson's friend, later told *Texas Monthly*. "But I know that something ain't right. If four black men had taken a mentally retarded white man to a party, made a monkey out of him, called him racial slurs, assaulted him, dumped him by the side of the road, and lied to the police about it, you can bet they would've gone to the penitentiary for a long, long time."

Many white residents of Linden welcomed the light sentences. A juror in one of the trials later said that Johnson "should have known better than to go drink beer with a bunch of white boys." Sympathy for the defendants ran strong among many in the community who didn't want to see the young men's lives stained by a serious conviction. "I don't think there was anything racial about it," Wilford Penny, who completed a sixth and final term as mayor at about the time of the sentencing, told Howard Witt of the *Chicago Tribune*. "These guys were drinking, and this guy liked to dance. I'm not surprised when they get to drinking and use the n-word. The black boy was somewhere he shouldn't have been, although they brought him out there."

Witt's article in the *Tribune* called national attention to the injustice and cast a harsh spotlight on racism in the piney woods of East Texas. The former mayor's casual use of the word "boy" to describe a 42-year-old black man spoke volumes about a rural county where, only three years prior to the crime against Johnson, a black man who had been dating a white woman was found hanging from a tree. In that case, the death was ruled a suicide. Seven years before that, another black man who was dating a white woman was found dead with a gunshot to the groin. That death was ruled as a hunting accident.

Witt's article also caught the eye of Morris Dees and other lawyers at the SPLC. The organization was already familiar with racial injustice in East

THE BILLY RAY JOHNSON CASE

Billy Ray Johnson was a 42-year-old black man with mental disabilities who lived in the East Texas town of Linden. One night in 2003, he was taken to an outdoor party where young white men and women were drinking beer around a bonfire. After being taunted with racial insults, Johnson was struck in the head and knocked unconscious, causing severe brain damage. Instead of taking Johnson to a hospital, several young men loaded his limp body in a pickup truck and dumped him along an isolated road, where he landed in a bed of fire ants. After the men were given slaps on the wrist by the local criminal justice system, the SPLC filed suit against those responsible.

VICTORY OVER RACISM IN EAST TEXAS
Morris Dees escorts Billy Ray Johnson from a courthouse after a nationally televised trial that cast a harsh spotlight on racism in the town of Linden, Texas. A jury of eleven whites and one African American awarded a $9 million judgment against the white men responsible for the brain injuries suffered by Johnson, who was struck on the head and left for dead. The town's previous mayor had said "the black boy was somewhere he shouldn't have been."

Texas. Seventeen years earlier, a black truck driver from Louisiana named Loyal Garner Jr. was beaten to death by lawmen in the town of Hemphill, about a hundred miles north of Linden along the state's eastern border. Garner had been arrested on a traffic charge on Christmas Day 1987. While in custody in the Sabine County Jail, he was dragged from his cell and savagely beaten. Left in his cell without medical care, he died two days later.

The SPLC sued the men and reached a significant monetary settlement to hold the lawmen accountable for the crime and to help provide financial security for Garner's wife and his six children. And, as the investigation unfolded, SPLC lawyers led by Richard Cohen and Texas pro bono attorney Glenn Perry discovered evidence that led prosecutors to file criminal charges against the Hemphill police chief and two sheriff's deputies. On May 3, 1990, an all-white jury found the men guilty of murder.

Dees, again with Perry's help, decided it was time to return to East Texas.

In September 2005, the SPLC filed suit against the four men responsible for Johnson's injuries. Two defendants reached settlements, and the case against the other two came to trial in April 2007. After four days of testimony in a nationally televised trial, a jury of eleven whites and one African American deliberated just four hours before returning a $9 million verdict for Johnson.

"Billy Ray is not an 'it,' like one of the defendants said," one juror said afterward. "He is a human being. We hope that our verdict sends a message to the nation about this community."

In a statement to reporters, Dees, who had delivered an impassioned closing argument, thanked the jury for being the "conscience of Cass County."

"The defendants in this case treated Billy Ray like trash," Dees said. "They broke his body and threw him in a ditch alongside a deserted road. The jury told all of Texas and, indeed, the entire country that Billy Ray is a human being who deserves to be treated with dignity, that the life of each of us—rich or poor, black or white, abled or disabled—is truly precious. It's a message, I hope, that we always remember." •

RACIAL INJUSTICE IN LOUISIANA

Morris Dees met with Louise Monroe on her front porch in Homer, Louisiana, where she lived with her husband, Bernard, for twenty-five years before he was shot to death by a white police officer on February 20, 2009. Two officers came onto the couple's property without provocation or a warrant during a family gathering, later claiming they thought a drug deal was in progress. One officer followed a son into the house and then shot the elder Monroe multiple times in the chest through the screen door as he walked toward it during the commotion. Though the officer claimed he was armed, witnesses said Monroe was carrying only a drink bottle. "Mr. Ben" was a well-liked retiree who had five children, eighteen grandchildren and fifteen great-grandchildren. The SPLC filed suit after a grand jury failed to charge the officer, leading to a confidential settlement with the town of Homer.

FREE THE JENA 6
LET LOOSE THE NOOSE
LET LOOSE THE NOOSE
INJUSTICE ANYWHERE IS A THREAT TO JUSTICE EVERYWHERE!
JIM CROW MUST GO!
JIM CROW MUST GO
WE ARE THE JENA 6
WE ARE THE JENA 6
WE ARE THE JENA 6
WE ARE THE JENA 6
FREE THE JENA 6
SOUTHERN

THE JENA SIX

In 2007, six black teens in the town of Jena, Louisiana, were charged with attempted murder in the beating of a white student amid racial tensions that began when white students hung nooses from a tree at the high school after black students sat under it. The severity of the charges, lodged by a white prosecutor in the predominantly white town, sparked outrage across the nation and drew thousands of demonstrators to Jena. SPLC lawyers coordinated the legal defense for the teens. In the end, five of the teens pleaded no contest to misdemeanor battery charges; each paid small fines and received a week of unsupervised probation. The other pleaded to second-degree battery as a juvenile. In October 2007, SPLC President Richard Cohen testified before the U.S. House Judiciary Committee about the racially charged events surrounding the Jena Six case.

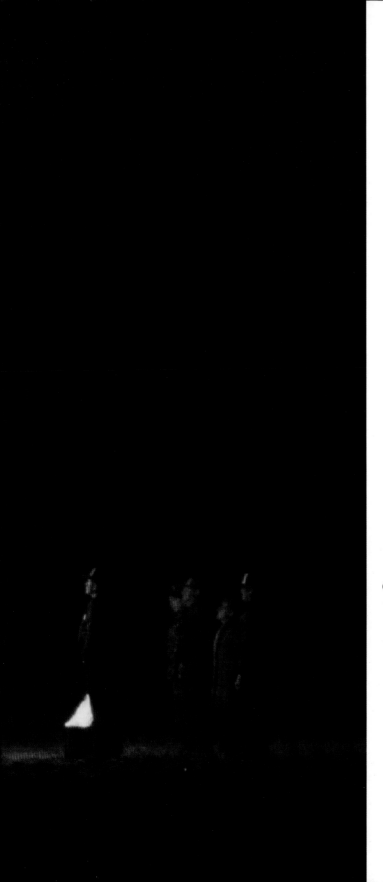

CHAPTER TWO

FIGHTING HATE GROUPS

MORRIS DEES REACHED FOR THE PHONE. It was just past 4 a.m.

The news was chilling.

This is the Montgomery Fire Department, Mr. Dees. The law center is on fire.

Dees pulled on his jeans and raced to the car. It was twenty-five miles to town, and by the time he arrived at his office on Hull Street the flames had been extinguished. A thick curtain of smoke hovered over the firefighters and policemen, the glow from streetlights piercing the gloom.

A small group of SPLC staffers huddled silently. Dees sat on a curb, his head sunk to his knees, sick at the thought of the destruction that awaited him inside, the thousands of pages of investigative files likely destroyed.

It took only minutes for investigators to reach a conclusion: Someone had broken a window to get in. They had poured an accelerant throughout the building and lit it.

The exterior of the building remained, but inside was a smoldering, sooty wreck of melted computers and blinds, charred carpet, fallen ceilings, and law books burned to a crisp.

The arsonist, obviously an amateur, had committed a mistake by failing to open windows. Starved of oxygen, the fire had largely burned itself out before it could completely consume the seven-thousand-square-foot building and its contents.

KLANSMEN TORCH THE SPLC OFFICE
In 1983, Klansmen broke into the SPLC office at night and set it on fire in retaliation for Morris Dees' lawsuit against the Invisible Empire over the beating of civil rights marchers in Decatur, Alabama. It would be the first of many plots to attack the SPLC office or assassinate Dees.

Some files had been strewn about and burned. Luckily, though, a set of fireproof file cabinets, just recently installed, had saved the bulk of them. Dees was elated. The contents were irreplaceable.

Shock and concern quickly turned to rage.

Who had done this? And why?

TO DEES AND HIS COLLEAGUES, it seemed obvious that the arson was the work of the Ku Klux Klan.

Proving it—and finding the culprit—was another matter.

Dees had received several threats from the Klan, dating back to his lawsuit to desegregate the Montgomery YMCA more than a decade earlier.

Six months before the fire, he had received a letter from Louis Beam, a volatile Klan leader in Texas, who challenged Dees to a duel—"to the death."

"You against me," wrote Beam, a former Vietnam War helicopter gunner. "No federal judges, no federal marshals, no FBI agents, not anyone except yourself and I. We go into the woods (your state or mine) and settle once and for all this enmity that exists between us. Two go in—one comes out."

Beam clearly had a bone to pick with Dees, one that began in a Houston courtroom two years earlier. He was part of a Klan resurgence that the SPLC had been monitoring for several years. Despite the new social order created by school desegregation

THE FIRST KLAN CASE
On March 26, 1979, about a hundred Klansmen attacked peaceful civil rights demonstrators with ax handles, bats and guns in Decatur, Alabama, leaving two black marchers shot and others injured. The attack reflected a resurgence of the Klan, which had been largely dormant since the end of the civil rights movement. Morris Dees brought suit against the Invisible Empire, led by Bill Wilkinson (above), in the first of many successful cases against Klan factions and other white supremacist groups.

and the enforcement of civil rights laws enacted in the 1960s, racism and resentment continued to burn hotly in the South. And the Klan, which had terrorized the black community for decades and waged a campaign of bombings, beatings and murders during the civil rights movement, had retreated but not gone away. Older Klan factions were now regaining strength even as new, militant leaders like Beam were emerging.

Blood had been shed.

In Greensboro, North Carolina, armed Klansmen and members of the American Nazi Party had attacked peaceful, anti-racist marchers on November 3, 1979. There were no police there to protect the marchers, and five were brazenly shot dead. Arrests were made, but the defendants were acquitted by all-white juries. The outcome showed that not much had changed in some Southern communities, where white juries had long refused to convict Klansmen for terrorist acts or hate crimes.

And in Decatur, Alabama, a civil rights rally on March 26, 1979—in support of a black man with mental disabilities who had been convicted of raping a white women—had turned bloody when about a hundred robe-wearing, hooded Klansmen attacked marchers with bats, axe handles and guns. Two black marchers were shot. Others were beaten bloody. Two Klansmen also were wounded by gunfire.

Dees had decided to file a lawsuit against the Invisible Empire, the Klan group responsible for the attack in Decatur. The suit represented a significant departure from the civil rights cases the SPLC had pursued over the previous decade, but Dees thought it necessary. A backlash to the gains of the civil rights movement was brewing, and the Klan was capitalizing on the resentment felt by a certain segment of whites, amid a period of economic stagnation, to build its ranks. "If we were going to

continue marching toward full equality, we needed to protect ourselves against a backlash from groups like the Klan along the way," Dees wrote later. "I was not turning my back on traditional civil rights cases. I was just not willing to sit back while our side suffered casualties."

Dees went further, establishing Klanwatch, a special investigative unit within the SPLC to monitor KKK activity and sue Klan groups for the violent acts of their members. (Klanwatch would later be named the Intelligence Project and gain international fame for monitoring a wide range of far-right extremist groups.)

In April 1981, five months after suing the Invisible Empire and its leader, Bill Wilkinson, over the Decatur attack, Dees and the SPLC took Beam to court as well, obtaining an injunction that stopped his Texas Knights of the Ku Klux Klan from intimidating Vietnamese fishermen who were competing with white fishermen on Galveston Bay.

But, despite Beam's suggestion to have a duel, it was the Decatur case that weighed on Dees' mind in the wake of the fire. The case was still winding its way through the courts, and Dees was trying to persuade federal prosecutors to file criminal conspiracy charges against Klansmen for the attack. The day before the fire, he had traveled to Birmingham to share incriminating photographs, tape-recorded confessions and other evidence with the U.S. Justice Department.

Dees suspected the fire was an attempt to destroy his voluminous Klan files. Over the next eighteen months, he and SPLC investigators, working with local prosecutors, would unravel the conspiracy to destroy the SPLC office.

In the meantime, they were about to embark on another Klan case that would make headlines around the world.

CONTINUED ON **PAGE 68**

THE EARLY YEARS OF FIGHTING HATE
In December 1989, the *Los Angeles Times* featured Morris Dees on the cover of its Sunday magazine and included this photo of Dees in his office. The SPLC founder had launched five major lawsuits against the Klan and, a month earlier, sued Tom Metzger and his White Aryan Resistance, based in California. The magazine's cover posed the question: "Can the Man Who Bankrupted the Klan Put California's White Supremacists Out of Business?" The answer was yes.

SOWING THE SEEDS OF HATE

A toddler in Klan regalia reaches out to touch his own reflection in the riot shield of a black state trooper in Gainesville, Georgia. Captured by Todd Robertson during a Klan rally, the picture has taken on a life of its own since it was published by *The Gainesville Times* in 1992. It has been used in textbooks and classroom exercises, often as a conversation starter for discussions about race and prejudice. The SPLC used it in a mural inside the Civil Rights Memorial Center to demonstrate how hate is passed from one generation to the next. The SPLC's Teaching Tolerance project also included the photo in its *Ten Ways to Fight Hate* guide for many years.

ON THE NIGHT OF MARCH 20, 1981, the Klansmen watching the 10 p.m. local news in Mobile, Alabama, were livid. A mistrial had just been declared in the case of Josephus Anderson, a black man accused of killing a white police officer after robbing a bank. A mostly black jury had not been able to reach a verdict.

"Goddam nigger got off," grumbled Henry Hays, the 28-year-old son of the highest-ranking Klan boss in South Alabama, Bennie Jack Hays.

A short time later, the younger Hays and another young Klansman quietly slipped into the night, mindful of the words spoken just two days earlier at a meeting of Klavern Unit 900 of the United Klans of America. "There ought be a damned nigger hung if this guy is turned loose," someone had said, to everyone's agreement.

A message needed to be sent—a clear one.

The two men drove around Mobile's north side, searching. An elderly black man was talking on a pay phone. They passed him by. Then they saw a figure walking alone in the dark.

Michael Donald had left his sister's house to pick up some cigarettes at a nearby store just a few minutes earlier. He, too, had been watching TV and was disappointed for a different reason: His hometown basketball team, the South Alabama Jaguars, had lost a close one.

As Donald walked, a 1979 black Buick Wildcat pulled up beside him. A stocky white man in the passenger seat asked directions to a nearby bar. Then he asked Donald, who was black, to come closer. When Donald leaned in, he found himself staring down the barrel of a .22-caliber pistol. He was ordered into the back seat. "I told him to be quiet and he would not be hurt," James "Tiger" Knowles, who was just 17, later testified in court.

Donald, 19, worked part-time in the mailroom at the local newspaper, the *Mobile Register*. The youngest of eight siblings, he lived at home with his mother, Beulah Mae, and was attending Carver State Technical College to learn masonry. He was known as a quiet young man who loved to play basketball and listen to music. He had spent the evening at his sister's house, as he often did. Now, his very life hung by a thread as the two white supremacists whisked him away from the neighborhood where he had grown up.

Knowles, who sat beside Donald in the red vinyl backseat of the Buick as Hays drove away from the city lights, ordered him to empty his pockets. Terrified, Donald begged for his life. "He kept saying, 'Please don't kill me,'" Knowles later recounted.

Hays finally stopped the car in a secluded, wooded area in nearby Baldwin County. They pushed Donald out.

It was now or never. Donald decided to fight—and did, like "a crazed madman," Knowles said. He knocked the gun from Knowles' hand, and it fired as it hit the ground. He tried to run. But Donald, who weighed just 160 pounds, was no match for the two Klansmen. After he was knocked to the ground, Hays retrieved a rope from the car. Knowles had already fashioned a noose, using the thirteen loops characteristic of a Klan knot. They managed to slip it around Donald's neck. "Henry put his foot on Michael's head to secure it to the ground so we could pull the rope tight," Knowles said. "And I grabbed the end of the rope. And Henry got a limb and he was hitting Donald with it."

As Donald struggled, rising repeatedly and being knocked back down, the Klansmen pummeled him with the limb, delivering more than a hundred blows. They tugged on the rope until Donald stopped struggling. To make sure he was dead, Hays slit his throat three times with a knife. They loaded the bloody, battered body into the trunk and took off. Back in Mobile, they showed off the corpse to another Klansman.

A few minutes after midnight, a cross was seen blazing on the lawn of the Mobile County Courthouse.

THE MICHAEL DONALD LYNCHING, 1981
In a grisly scene right out of the Deep South's darkest past, 19-year-old Michael Donald was found hanging from a tree in a Mobile, Alabama, neighborhood on March 20, 1981. Two Klansmen were convicted of murder, but Morris Dees believed that other members of the notorious United Klans of America were involved in a larger conspiracy to kill the teen. He filed suit against the group, initiating a novel legal strategy that would destroy the organization.

Beulah Mae hardly slept that night. Her son had not come home. And Donald's sister had not seen him since he left to get cigarettes.

A little after 5 a.m., Michael's sister arrived bearing terrible news. A badly beaten body had been found hanging from a camphor tree on Herndon Avenue, a neighborhood where both whites and African Americans lived. The break of dawn revealed a grisly tableau right out of the Deep South's darkest past, the body of a black man dangling from a rope.

The location was significant. Bennie Jack Hays, a "grand titan" whose territory covered the lower half of Alabama, owned several rental properties on Herndon Avenue, including a house right across the street from the tree that held Donald's body. Living in an apartment in that house was a killer, his son Henry.

Just four days after the murder, three white men were arrested. But they were the wrong men, and a grand jury refused to indict them after a key witness' testimony was shown to be false. Two years passed before authorities broke the case. Then, in June 1983, the FBI slapped handcuffs on the two men who murdered Donald. To avoid the death penalty, Knowles quickly spilled his guts. He pleaded guilty to federal charges of violating Donald's civil rights and was sentenced to life in prison in exchange for testifying against his partner. Hays, however, denied the charge and was put on trial for murder in December 1983.

Morris Dees and Bill Stanton, who ran the SPLC's Klanwatch program, sat in the courtroom and watched the four-day trial. Stanton hoped to gather information by posing as a Texas Klansman who was there to support Hays. Dees hoped to hear testimony that would implicate other Klansmen in a conspiracy.

The moment they were waiting for came when Knowles testified that Donald was killed solely because he was black and that the purpose was to "show the strength of the Klan ... to show that they were still here in Alabama."

While the jury deliberated, Dees and Stanton began the three-hour drive back to Montgomery, but not before standing for a long time in silence at the camphor tree on Herndon Avenue. On the ride home, Dees began to formulate a novel legal theory to destroy the United Klans of America, a way to hold the entire organization and its leadership accountable for the savage killing of Michael Donald.

The SPLC had already scored a legal victory against Louis Beam in Texas. But this case was different.

The state prosecutors who tried Hays believed that he and Knowles had acted alone. Dees didn't buy it.

"These bastards were agents of the Klan," Dees said. "Why can't we sue the Klan like you'd sue any corporation liable for the acts of its agents?"

"I've never heard of the Klan being sued like that," Stanton said.

Neither had Dees. For one thing, corporations typically weren't liable for the criminal actions of their agents.

Back in Mobile, the jury deliberated four and a half hours before finding Hays guilty of capital murder on the strength of Knowles' testimony and plenty of corroborating evidence. The jury recommended life in prison without the possibility of parole. The judge saw differently and sentenced Hays to death.

The obstacles notwithstanding, Dees decided to move forward. The investigation began, one that would go far beyond that of the prosecutors.

Six months after Hays' trial, on June 14, 1984, the SPLC and Beulah Mae Donald's attorney, state Senator Michael Figures, filed suit in federal court against the United Klans of America Inc., its Mobile klavern, Bennie Jack Hays, Henry Hays, Tiger Knowles and a handful of other United Klans members.

The case wasn't about money. None of the defendants had much. And the group itself had few assets other than its national headquarters outside of Tuscaloosa, a 7,200-square-foot building owned by a

BEULAH MAE DONALD
Beulah Mae Donald worried all night when her youngest son, Michael, 19, went to his sister's house and never came home. At 5 a.m. she received the heartbreaking news that his badly beaten body had been found hanging from a tree. Five months after the criminal trial of one of the murderers, the SPLC filed suit on her behalf against the United Klans of America.

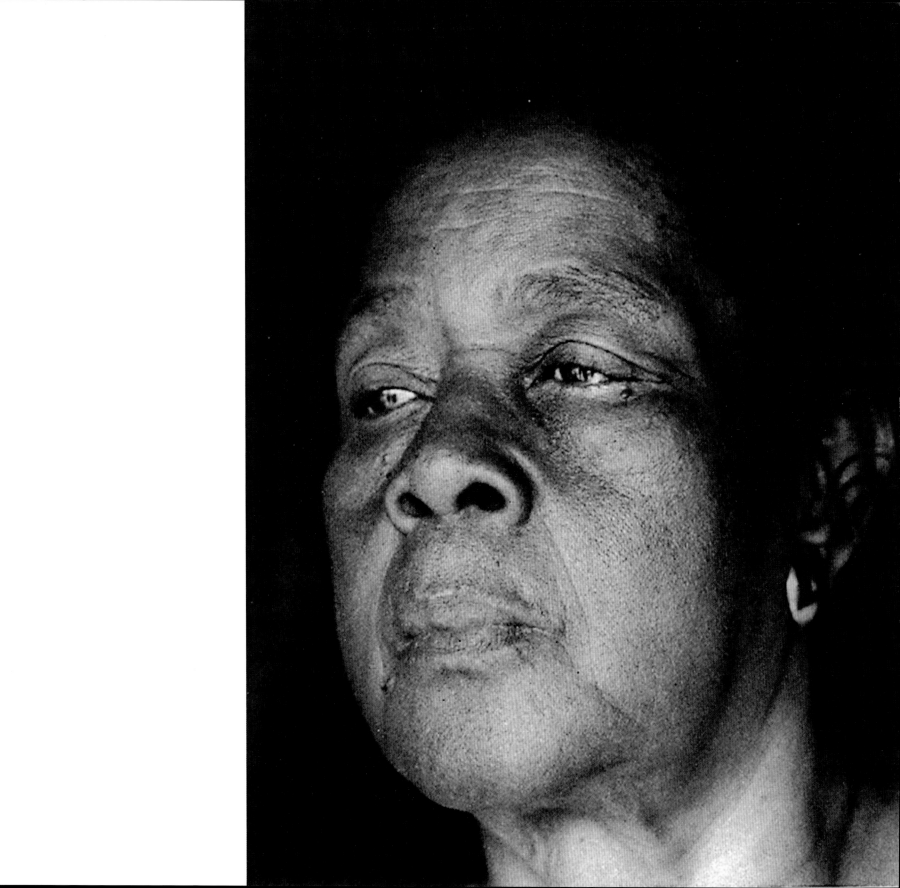

UNITED KLANS—A HISTORY OF VIOLENCE

The group responsible for the Michael Donald murder was among the most notorious of the Klan groups operating in America and had committed some of the most heinous crimes of the civil rights era, including the beating of Freedom Riders in several Alabama cities, the murder of civil rights activist Viola Liuzzo, the bombing of Birmingham's 16th Street Baptist Church, and the murder of Lt. Col. Lemuel Penn, an Army reservist, in Georgia.

thinly disguised United Klans front called the Anglo-Saxon Club Inc.

"Mr. Dees," Beulah Mae Donald said, "no amount of money is going to bring back Michael or make my heart ache any less. That's not why I agreed to this suit. You just find all the people who killed my baby, and let the world know, and I'll be able to go to my grave."

Dees and the legal team figured that for their theory to prevail in court they would need to prove that the United Klans had a history of violence against African Americans, that the Mobile chapter was tied to the national group, and that the murder was the result of a conspiracy carried out with the knowledge and consent of United Klans officials.

As they interviewed and deposed Klansmen who had attended meetings prior to the murder, they began to unravel the conspiracy and to pierce the veil of secrecy surrounding Klan activities. Dees soon had strong evidence to show that Bennie Jack Hays, the grand titan, had been at the center of the conspiracy.

Among others deposed by Dees was Gary Thomas Rowe, the Klansman and FBI informant who had been in the car on March 25, 1965, when United Klans members shot and killed Viola Liuzzo, a 39-year-old white woman from Detroit, as she ferried civil rights marchers back to Selma after the pivotal Selma-to-Montgomery voting rights march. Rowe provided key details of United Klans violence and linked it to the group's top leaders.

The murder of Liuzzo, a mother of five, was one of the keys to illustrating the group's record of violence. But it wasn't the first or the last such act. The fact was, the United Klans was among the most violent of the Klan networks operating around the country. It had been formed from several Klan factions by Robert Shelton in 1961 at the height of the civil rights movement, when white supremacists were waging a terror campaign to intimidate African Americans and civil rights activists.

A prominent Klan leader, Shelton had orchestrated the Klan attacks on the Freedom Riders in Anniston, Birmingham and Montgomery in 1961. Two years later, in September 1963, Robert Chambliss and other United Klans members bombed the 16th Street Baptist Church in Birmingham, killing four young black girls. Then, in July 1964, members shot and killed U.S. Army Reservist Lt. Col. Lemuel Penn, a black man chosen at random as he traveled along the highway in Georgia.

These crimes showed a definite pattern, but Dees figured they might seem like ancient history to a jury. He needed something more recent. And he found it. In 1979, thirteen members of the group had been convicted on federal charges for shooting into the home of a local NAACP official in Childersburg, Alabama.

Dees had the missing link he needed.

When the SPLC case came to trial in March 1987, Tiger Knowles told his story once again, recounting the murder in chilling detail—but also providing key details of Klan structure, operations, chain of command, and the conspiracy itself. Knowles testified that the plot was conceived by Bennie Jack Hays and approved by the membership at the klavern meeting held two days before the murder. The testimony of other Klansmen backed up his account.

Dees asked Knowles why Donald was killed.

"Because he was—black people shouldn't be on juries ... it was strictly white supremacy," Knowles replied, referring to the jury's inability to return a verdict in the Josephus Anderson murder trial.

As part of its legal strategy, the SPLC team had obtained from Bennie Jack Hays a Klan charter showing that Klavern Unit 900 was indeed under the command of Shelton's national organization. Knowles testified that he reported to Hays and that Hays reported directly to Shelton.

The evidence was falling into place to advance Dees' legal theory. Now, he needed to show that the United Klans officially advocated violence.

DONALD'S KILLERS PUNISHED
Morris Dees used a 1979 edition of *The Fiery Cross*, a United Klans publication, to demonstrate to jurors in the Michael Donald case that the organization encouraged violence against African Americans. The evidence was instrumental in establishing that the Klan group itself, not just the two men convicted in criminal court, was culpable for the murder. James "Tiger" Knowles (far right), just 19 when he helped kill Donald, pleaded guilty to federal charges and received a life sentence. He later described the crime in graphic detail to the jury that convicted Henry Hays (far left), who died in Alabama's electric chair in 1997. Evidence gathered by the SPLC was used by prosecutors to indict Bennie Jack Hays (third from left)—Henry's father and the "grand titan" in South Alabama—for his role in the conspiracy. The elder Hays went to prison for fraud after burning down his house to collect insurance money, then collapsed during his murder trial and died before he could be retried.

With Knowles on the stand, Dees produced a 1979 edition of the *Fiery Cross*, the United Klans' newspaper. In it, there was a cartoon of a white man saying, "It's terrible the way blacks are being treated. All whites should work to give the blacks what they deserve." Below the cartoon, there was an arrow and the words "Turn page." The next page contained a crude drawing, typical of the racist depictions found in white supremacist propaganda, of a black man with a noose around his neck.

"Now when you saw this piece of information, how did you interpret that coming from Robert Shelton, editor in chief, as a Klan official?" Dees asked.

"That's what blacks deserved—to be hung," Knowles replied. "And that we should go out and since this was a publication of the Klan telling us what we should do and telling the Klan's beliefs, that's what we should do, go out and hang black people."

In the 2011 book *Thirteen Loops*, author B.J. Hollars writes that Dees' closing argument "hit the jury like a wallop."

Dees told the jury not to return a verdict based on the Klan's racism. "In this country you have the right to have unpopular beliefs just as long as you don't turn those beliefs into violent action that interferes with somebody else's rights," Dees said. "But they put a rope around Michael Donald's neck and treated him to an awful death on a dirt road in Baldwin County so that they could get out their message.

"You have an opportunity to send a different message. A message that will ring out from the top of this courthouse and be heard all over Alabama and all over the United States—that an all-white jury from the heart of the South will not tolerate racial violence in any way, shape or form."

With tears trickling down his face, Dees continued, "No matter what you decide, Michael Donald will take his place in history along with others whose lives were lost in the struggle for human rights. And when the final roll is called in heaven—when they call Dr. Martin Luther King, and Medgar Evers, and Viola Liuzzo—they will also call Michael Donald. I hope the verdict you reach will also go down in history on the side of justice."

On February 12, 1987, nearly six years after the murder, the jury deliberated for four and a half hours before rendering a $7 million verdict against the United Klans of America.

Newspapers across the country trumpeted the landmark verdict. During the dark days of the civil rights movement, all-white juries in the Deep South had routinely refused to hold accountable those who terrorized and murdered African Americans in the name of white supremacy. Now, one had sent a striking message: It was a new day.

The New York Times, in an editorial, called the verdict "monumental" and noted that it was "the first time a Klan organization has been held financially liable because it was so linked to violence committed by its members. The Alabama verdict gives a new meaning to the old slogan: those who sanction brutal crimes must pay."

"That these six white Alabamans voted to stick it to the Klan is reaffirmation that, while echoes of the South's segregationist past can still be heard, the decent majority wants no part of it," *The Philadelphia Inquirer* wrote. Added *The Atlanta Constitution*, "Maybe financial bankruptcy will prove more lethal to the Klan than its moral bankruptcy."

Shortly afterward, the keys to the United Klans' headquarters building arrived in Dees' mail. A little more than $50,000 was recovered from the sale, and Beulah Mae Donald was able to buy a small house, the first she had ever owned. She died just a year and a half after the trial, at age 67, secure in the knowledge that her son's killers had paid for their crime.

CONTINUED ON **PAGE 80**

SOUTHERN POVERTY LAW CENTER
400 Washington Avenue
Montgomery, Alabama 36195

Non Profit Org.
U.S. Postage
PAID
The Southern Poverty
Law Center

Law Report

A publication of the Southern Poverty Law Center and its Klanwatch Project   March/April 1987

Jury Awards Mrs. Donald $7 Million

For First Time, A Jury Finds KKK Liable for Members' Violent Acts

MOBILE, Ala. -- The United Klans of America and six of its members have been ordered by an all-white jury to pay $7 million in damages to Mrs. Beulah Mae Donald, whose teen-aged son, Michael, was brutally murdered by the Klan here in 1981.

It marks the first time in history that a Ku Klux Klan group — the organization itself — has been found liable by a jury for the actions of its members. Center attorneys believe the case sets a precedent for other victims of Klan violence.

The verdict was handed down in a civil suit brought on behalf of

statutes, accused the six Klansmen of conspiring to murder a black man in retaliation for a mostly black jury's failure to convict a black defendant who was on trial in 1981 for killing a white officer in a totally unrelated case.

Two Klansmen were arrested for killing Donald following a long federal investigation and are now serving time in prison for the murder (See story, page 3).

Evidence in the SPLC lawsuit demonstrated that the murder plot was conceived by three Klansmen: Bennie Jack Hays, a titan or regional officer and the highest-

ALABAMA JURY DEMOLISHES KLAN, 1987

Nearly six years after Klansmen murdered Michael Donald to terrorize the black community in Mobile, Alabama, an all-white jury signaled a new day in the state by delivering a $7 million verdict against the United Klans of America. The group was destroyed, and to satisfy the judgment it was forced to turn over its headquarters building in Tuscaloosa. With the $50,000 in proceeds, Beulah Mae Donald was able to buy the first house she had ever owned. In 2006, the Mobile City Council voted to rename Herndon Avenue, the street where Donald's body was found, in honor of the slain teen.

MICHAEL DONALD'S FAMILY VISITS MEMORIAL
On March 20, 2009—the twenty-eighth anniversary of Michael Donald's murder by Klansmen—about sixty family members and friends gathered for a reunion hosted by the SPLC at the Civil Rights Memorial Center. Cecilia Perry, Donald's sister, wrote to thank the SPLC: "We are humbled that Michael and my mother's lives are remembered in your facility. We pray that God will continue to bless you in your fight for equality in America."

But the civil trial would not be the end of the case. Prosecutors would use the evidence gathered by Dees and the SPLC's legal team to indict Bennie Jack Hays and his son-in-law, Frank Cox, for their roles in the conspiracy to murder Michael Donald. Cox was convicted and sentenced to ninety-nine years but was released in 2000. Hays went to prison for fraud after he was convicted of burning down his house to collect insurance money to pay lawyers. He collapsed during the first trial on the murder conspiracy charges and then died before he could be retried. His son, Henry Hays, was executed in Alabama's electric chair on June 6, 1997, becoming the first white man to die for killing a black man in Alabama since 1913.

The United Klans of America, the creation of a 1950s-era Klan boss who promoted hate and terrorism, was dead.

IN 1983, AS AUTHORITIES IN MOBILE were closing in on the Klansmen who killed Michael Donald, Klansmen in North Carolina were beginning a campaign of intimidation aimed at a black prison guard named Bobby Person. The previous October, Person filed discrimination complaints with a state board alleging bias in promotion practices after he and another black guard applied for supervisory jobs at the Moore County Correctional Unit.

On May 30, Klansmen burned a cross in Person's lawn. They littered his property and a neighboring churchyard with racist literature and scratched "KKK" on his father's pickup. Soon after, his wife and children were harassed while driving to town.

Then, during the afternoon of October 12, a pickup truck pulled up in front of Person's double-wide trailer. A white man, who Person recognized as a fellow guard at the prison, stood in the truck bed holding a rifle. No shots were fired, but as the truck sped away the Klansman in the back made a Nazi salute.

At dusk, the riders returned with two additional passengers. A man dressed in camouflage and holding a .22-caliber rifle called for Person to come out. As his wife and children huddled inside, Person, a former infantryman, grabbed a shotgun and ran out. One of the men yelled, "Come out from behind that tree, nigger, and I'll whip your ass." Person challenged the men to come into his yard, but they left again. As they drove off, one of the men shouted that they would "keep coming back until you straighten up."

The harassment continued, and the following spring Person met with Dees to discuss a lawsuit. "If you file suit, they might come back and burn your house down," Dees told him.

"If I'm going to have to live like I'm living, I might as well live with it burned down," Person replied.

Dees could not have guessed at the time that the case would reach far beyond the incidents that terrorized Person and his family.

Other acts of Klan intimidation in the area had already caught the eye of the SPLC's Klanwatch investigators. A cross was burned in the yard of a white woman suspected of dating a black man; a local business owner was told by Klansmen to stop hiring black people. Something was going on in eastern North Carolina.

The SPLC soon discovered that a former Green Beret, a Vietnam War veteran named Glenn Miller, had recently settled on a farm in Angier, about 25 miles south of Raleigh. He had quickly established the Carolina Knights of the Ku Klux Klan.

Miller, who was 42, was a former member of the National Socialist Party of America, a Nazi organization, and been present during the deadly clash between white supremacists and anti-racist activists in Greensboro. Like Louis Beam in Texas, he represented the new breed of Klan leaders. He preferred fatigues to traditional Klan robes and organized his group like a military unit. He was not averse to publicity, either.

KLAN INTIMIDATION IN NORTH CAROLINA, 1983
Prison guard Bobby Person was suing the state for racial discrimination when Klansmen burned a cross in his yard and began harassing his family. After the intimidation escalated, he met with Morris Dees to consider a lawsuit. It was the beginning of the case against ex-Green Beret Glenn Miller and his paramilitary group, the Carolina Knights of the Ku Klux Klan—one of the most harrowing cases Dees and other lawyers at the SPLC would ever try.

Miller began holding rallies and marches on a near-weekly basis up and down the Atlantic Seaboard. He announced his goal was to create a Carolina Free State, which would be an "all-white nation within the bounds of North and South Carolina." His enemies, he said, were "niggers" and Jews.

SPLC investigators began to catch wind of paramilitary training on the farm in Angier and learned that Miller boasted of having supporters at Fort Bragg, a nearby Army base and home to a large contingent of U.S. Special Forces. Suddenly, the Person case took on a new, frightening dimension. But to bring down Miller, Dees needed to link the harassment of Person to the Carolina Knights. That didn't take long. The Klansman who led the intimidation—Person's fellow prison guard—admitted during a deposition that he was part of Miller's "elite force," a unit he compared favorably—and hyperbolically—to the special forces at Fort Bragg.

On June 5, 1984, Dees filed suit against Miller, the Carolina Knights and several others—demanding they stop intimidating African Americans and cease all paramilitary training. It was the beginning of one of the most harrowing cases that Dees, his chief legal deputy, Richard Cohen, and the others at the SPLC would ever try.

They did not know it at the time, but Miller was connected to "The Order," a white nationalist terrorist organization whose members assassinated Denver radio host Alan Berg just thirteen days after the SPLC filed suit against the Carolina Knights.

The leader of The Order, Robert Mathews, had also given Miller $200,000 in cash—a fraction of the $3.8 million stolen during an armored car robbery. It was later revealed that Dees was at the top of The Order's hit list and that Mathews had reportedly offered an Alabama Klansman $50,000 to carry out the hit.

Dees knew little about Miller's network or his relationship with The Order, but given the litany of threats he had received since he first began suing Klan groups he wasn't taking any chances. When the SPLC lawyers flew into Raleigh to conduct depositions in November, they registered under false names at their hotel and wore bulletproof vests. At the courthouse, they were forced to push through a mob of Klansmen wearing army fatigues and combat boots, some of whom were snapping pictures of them and muttering obscenities. Randall Williams, who worked in the SPLC's Klanwatch unit, was arrested for assaulting a Klan photographer. The charge was absurd, and Williams was later acquitted.

As the day wore on, tensions rose. One Klansman stuck a camera in Dees' face, and Dees responded with a forearm to his head. After lunch, the SPLC team decided to leave town. They knew they needed to be careful. "However dangerous it was to stay," Dees later wrote, "it seemed even more dangerous to leave. We'd make better targets out on the open road, away from the courthouse. It wasn't too hard to imagine our car followed by a convoy of armed Carolina Knights. We were armed, too. A shoot-out seemed quite possible, Greensboro redux."

Dees requested a police escort to the airport, but the state troopers, the county sheriff and the local police all refused. So Dees devised a plan. After a deposition ended at 2 p.m., he announced that the SPLC team needed to meet in private before the next one. Earlier, they had found a back door, and they decided to use it. Having departed safely from the courthouse, Dees and the others drove to the airport without incident, later learning that Miller had waited more than an hour for them to return. By the time the Klan leader realized he had been tricked, the SPLC lawyers were safely in the air.

The trip had been fruitful. Dees obtained explosive information: Marines from Camp Lejeune in Jacksonville, North Carolina, were leading Miller's Klansmen in paramilitary maneuvers and teaching

GLENN MILLER AND THE ORDER
Glenn Miller spent twenty years in the Army, including two tours in Vietnam, but was forced to retire because of his white supremacist activities. He bought a farm in Angier, North Carolina, and used it as a base for his paramilitary Klan group, which he wanted to model after Hitler's Nazi Party. Miller represented a new breed of Klan leader, preferring military fatigues to traditional Klan robes and training his followers in military tactics. At one point, he received $200,000 in cash from the leader of The Order, a racist terrorist group whose members assassinated Jewish Denver radio host Alan Berg (above) in 1984. Morris Dees was also on The Order's hit list.

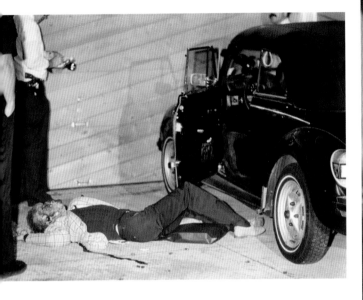

them combat techniques. Now there was solid evidence that active-duty military personnel were involved.

Later that month, while Dees was in Mobile for the Donald case, the FBI called SPLC security officials to warn that a white supremacist group had dispatched assassins to Alabama to kill Dees. An FBI informant had learned of the plot after infiltrating The Order. A week later, guards at Dees' farm south of Montgomery spotted two men with flashlights in a pasture near his house. They escaped before they could be apprehended. A few days later, Mathews was killed in a shootout with FBI officials. It didn't occur to Dees that Mathews might have been the one who ordered the assassination.

On December 10, two days after Mathews was killed and just a week after the first intrusion, guards again spotted two men.

It was dark out, and Dees was decorating the Christmas tree with his 14-year-old daughter, Ellie, when he heard the voice of a guard over the security team's radio: "Jesus Christ, there's someone out there. There's someone on the property."

A guard inside the house hustled Dees and Ellie into a safe room. Dees grabbed a Berretta and handed his daughter a .22-caliber pistol, hoping that neither would be needed. The voice on the radio came back: "There were two of them. I think I see one in the bushes."

Dees put his arm around Ellie and held her as she trembled. "First they burn down your law office, now they come after you," she said. "Why do you do the cases you do, Daddy? I don't understand."

"Just hold on to me and close your eyes, and it'll be over in a little while, I promise," Dees said, pulling her tighter.

The guard outside had been sitting in his pickup with the lights turned off when he saw two men cross the dirt road leading to the house. Both were carrying guns. When he drove toward them, they ran into the woods.

An hour later, two sheriff's deputies and an FBI agent arrived. While searching the area, one of the deputies found a piece of camouflage cloth along the driveway.

It was after 1 a.m. when the officers left. Later, as Dees tried to sleep, Ellie's words echoed in his mind. She had a point. He was financially secure. He was healthy and blessed with a loving family. He had everything. Why risk it all?

He thought also of Beulah Mae Donald, who had lost her son Michael to a Klan outfit that had terrorized so many, whose members had cold-bloodedly murdered the four girls in the 16th Street Baptist Church—Addie Mae Collins, Denise McNair, Carole Robertson and Cynthia Wesley.

In the morning, he would tell Ellie he wanted her to accompany him to court when he sought justice for Ms. Donald.

He knew he couldn't turn back now.

THE INVESTIGATION INTO THE FIRE at the SPLC office twisted and turned for eighteen months.

Early on, Dees had focused his attention on a man named Joe Garner, a local Klan leader who was, ironically, the chief of a volunteer fire department in Snowdoun, a tiny farming community just ten miles south of town. Six weeks before the fire, Dees had taken Garner's deposition for the Decatur case, in which the SPLC was alleging an ongoing conspiracy among Klansmen in Alabama to harm African Americans. Just days before the fire, Dees had caught wind that Garner had called him a "son of a bitch" who was "after him." Garner had another reason to retaliate against Dees: When he had earlier run for sheriff, the SPLC had given the local newspaper a photograph of Garner speaking at a Klan rally.

Dees also suspected the involvement of two brothers, aged 19 and 20, who lived in a room behind the store Garner ran in Snowdoun. A solid clue came

PHOTOGRAPHS HELP SOLVE ARSON
Two of the Klansmen who were arrested for conspiring to burn the SPLC office—Joe Garner (1) and Tommy Downs (2)—were part of this January 1, 1980, march in Birmingham, Alabama. After Downs denied being a member of the Klan during the arson investigation, Morris Dees used this photograph to persuade local prosecutors to call Downs before a grand jury. Presented with the evidence, Downs confessed to the crime. Earlier, the SPLC had provided a photograph of Garner at a Klan rally to the local newspaper when Garner was running for sheriff.

KLANSMEN ARRESTED IN SPLC ARSON
On December 12, 1984, state prosecutor Jimmy Evans (center) announces a
Montgomery, Alabama, grand jury's indictment of the Klansmen responsible for setting
fire to the SPLC office eighteen months earlier. In the foreground are confiscated explosives that the Klan intended to use against civil rights marchers. The ringleader of the
arson plot—Joe Garner, a local Klan leader who was, ironically, the chief of a small rural
fire department near Montgomery—was sentenced to fifteen years in prison. The two
who carried it out, Tommy Downs and Charles Bailey, received three-year sentences.

from Dees' friend who ran a garage across the street from Garner's store. He told Dees that the older brother, Tommy Downs, had left a garden sprayer in his shop that smelled of gasoline. At the same time, SPLC investigators were able to confirm that Downs was a member of the Klan.

Another break came when Dees set up a ruse to elicit a confession from Downs. A friend named James Killough hired the brothers to help build a shed at the garage across the street from their residence. Soon, the talk turned to "race mixing," and from there to Dees. "That's the son of a bitch who's causing our problems," Killough said.

The conversation continued later over beers at a local tavern, when Tommy Downs blurted out, "You know, we took care of that Dees fellow."

"What do you mean?" Killough asked.

"This guy I work for, Joe Garner, we went down there and burned that office."

The Downs brothers were hauled before a grand jury, but they denied knowing anything about the fire. Dees then subpoenaed Garner, the Downs brothers and one of their friends, Charles Bailey, as part of the Decatur investigation. Again, they denied everything. But Bailey seemed nervous.

The investigation hit a dead end. Little new would be learned for more than a year. But fortunes turned in December 1984, when the SPLC obtained a photograph of Tommy Downs at a Klan rally with Joe Garner. Both were wearing robes. Dees knew he had the leverage he needed to put pressure on Downs.

Downs was hauled back before a grand jury, and he again denied being a member of the Klan. But when presented with the photograph and told he could face five years in prison for perjury, he broke down and confessed that he and Charles Bailey had been hired by Garner to set the fire. There was more work to be done to corroborate the story, but the facts soon fell in line.

Under pressure, Garner told everything to the FBI. He said that in March 1983, four months before the fire, Louis Beam and Klan leader Thom Robb had visited him and asked questions about Dees. Beam had called the SPLC founder "scum" for not answering his challenge of a duel. "It's a damn shame that a man like Morris Dees can jog up and down these streets and still breathe this air," Beam had said.

But the main reason the fire was set was to retaliate for the Decatur case and to destroy SPLC files. At one point, tired of Dees' harassment, Garner offered Bailey $1,000 to kill the SPLC founder.

Garner told the FBI that on the night of the fire Downs and Bailey met him at his store, where they filled up the garden sprayer with gasoline. Garner dropped them off four blocks from the SPLC office. They reached the office by crawling through the sewer system. Downs went inside and set the fire while Bailey stood lookout. Then, they left, again, through the sewer system.

All three were indicted, and all pleaded guilty. Garner was sentenced to fifteen years; Downs and Bailey each received three-year sentences.

IN JANUARY 1985, the SPLC lawyers returned to Raleigh to take Glenn Miller's deposition. This time, they requested and were allowed to use the federal courthouse, knowing that U.S. marshals would not allow Miller's men to crowd the hallways. They also obtained a protective order. Miller unsuccessfully sought a protective order, too, citing the assault charge against the SPLC's Williams and claiming, falsely, that the SPLC had orchestrated a burglary at his home and the theft of Klan documents. As the deposition progressed, Dees noticed that Miller's hands were shaking. He seemed nervous and timid, compared to his earlier bravado.

"If I had known at the time that Miller was afraid we might find out Robert Mathews had visited him twice in 1984 and had given him $200,000 in cash, I might have understood why the grand dragon looked like a mouse," Dees said. "All I knew was that a window of opportunity had opened."

Dees jumped. On a legal pad, he sketched out a settlement: The Carolina Knights would cease operating as a paramilitary organization, which violated several state laws, and would no longer harass, intimidate or threaten African Americans. Miller agreed to everything.

Dees didn't believe Miller would live up to the settlement terms. But if he didn't, the SPLC could seek to have him jailed for criminal contempt. And that, Dees reasoned, wouldn't be such a bad outcome.

True to form, Miller sent out a press release a month later announcing the Carolina Knights had been disbanded but that he had formed a new group called the White Patriot Party. Its goal was the same: the "unification of white people." He vowed to operate it peacefully—unless the federal government infringed on his rights, in which case he would resort to "underground revolutionary tactics ... with the armed resources at our disposal."

Over the next year, the SPLC kept a watchful eye on Miller's organization and obtained two photographs of active-duty Marines working with White Patriot Party members. The SPLC knew that Miller's talk of overthrowing the government and establishing a white homeland was pure fantasy. But, as a former special forces soldier with a cache of weapons and, now, an estimated twenty-four hundred followers, Miller was capable of terrorist acts that could kill and maim a large number of people. Dees did two things. First, he sent the photographs and other evidence to Defense Secretary Caspar Weinberger, with a plea

CONTINUED ON **PAGE 92**

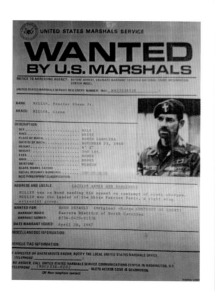

MILLER RETURNS WITH NEW GROUP
After he signed an agreement with the SPLC to stop operating his Carolina Knights as a paramilitary organization, Glenn Miller formed a new group— the White Patriot Party—and resumed his activities, using training and weapons, including anti-tank rockets stolen by active-duty military personnel. Miller staged numerous public rallies in the Carolinas, often flying the Confederate battle flag, before he became a wanted man.

MILLER CONVICTED OF CONTEMPT

After obtaining photographic evidence of Marines working with Glenn Miller, Morris Dees and Richard Cohen served as special U.S. prosecutors to bring criminal contempt charges against the volatile Vietnam veteran. Miller was convicted but went underground and called for his followers to kill Dees. A SWAT team flushed him out of a trailer in Missouri, and he spent three years in prison on charges related to his threat. In 2014, at 73, Miller burst back into the spotlight when he attacked a Jewish community center and a Jewish retirement home in Overland Park, Kansas, shooting three people to death.

to take action to prevent soldiers from participating in white supremacist organizations. Then, he filed a motion to hold Miller in contempt of court.

The problem was that Dees, a civilian, could not prosecute the criminal contempt case against Miller. But that obstacle was overcome when the U.S. attorney agreed to take the case and appoint Dees as a special prosecutor to assist him. So, in July 1986, Dees and Cohen returned to Raleigh for a jury trial against Miller, this time under heavy security provided by U.S. marshals. Miller's men, now wearing civilian clothes, crowded the courtroom. "One shot is all it takes, Dees," someone shouted as the SPLC founder entered. It was no idle threat; the night before the trial, someone had broken the jaw of a former soldier who was poised to testify against Miller. Despite the setback, a former Marine—who had been discharged because he wouldn't give up his membership in the White Patriot Party after Dees' disclosures to the Pentagon—admitted that paramilitary training had continued following the earlier court settlement. Another witness testified that he had procured weapons and explosives, including thirteen armor-penetrating anti-tank rockets, from military personnel on behalf of Miller, even after the settlement. He also said he received a duffel bag full of cash as payment for conducting training intended to help "create a paramilitary guerrilla unit for later use in establishing a White Southland."

The jury took six hours to deliver a unanimous guilty verdict. Sentencing was delayed for several months, but the judge ordered Miller and his associate, Stephen Miller (no relation), to disassociate themselves from the White Patriot Party and to avoid any contact with white supremacists. Miller was later sentenced to a year in prison, with six months of that term suspended. Within a month, Miller's group was disbanded.

But in 1987, while out on bond as he awaited the appeal of his conviction, Miller disappeared and went underground. He issued a declaration exhorting "Aryan warriors of The Order" to kill "our enemies," and established a point system for each kill. The targets were: "Niggers (1), White race traitors (10), Jews (10), Judges (50) Morris Seligman Dees (888)." He signed the statement "Glenn Miller, loyal member of 'The Order.'"

The FBI soon caught up with Miller and four other Klansmen in Springfield, Missouri, where a SWAT team used tear gas to flush him out of a mobile home. Authorities found hand grenades, automatic weapons, thousands of rounds of ammunition, the explosive C-4 and $14,000 in cash. He and the others were indicted for conspiracy to acquire stolen military weapons, explosives and equipment, and for planning robberies and the assassination of Dees. Miller served three years in federal prison after pleading guilty to a weapons charge and to sending a threat through the mail. As part of his plea deal, he testified against fourteen white supremacist leaders in a 1988 sedition trial that ended in acquittals.

Miller never again regained his stature within the white-power movement and was seen as a traitor to its cause. For decades, he continued to publish racist commentary, particularly on the Internet. Then, in April 2014, while living in Missouri at age 73 and going by the name Glenn Frazier Cross, he was arrested after attacking a Jewish community center and retirement home in Overland Park, Kansas, where he shot to death three people he apparently thought were Jewish. None were.

The Miller case was over, but it represented the beginning of a long campaign by the SPLC to ensure that the U.S. military wouldn't be a breeding ground for highly trained, violent white supremacists.

CONTINUED ON **PAGE 97**

THE SKINHEAD MURDER OF MULUGETA SERAW, 1988

Tom Metzger, a Klan "grand dragon" in California and a former disciple of David Duke, in the 1980s formed a neo-Nazi group he called the White Aryan Resistance, or WAR, and began recruiting violent racist skinheads to be the "shock troops" of a coming revolution. In 1988, skinheads advised by WAR attacked and beat to death Ethiopian graduate student Mulugeta Seraw on the street in Portland, Oregon—a crime praised by Metzger as their "civic duty." The SPLC sued Metzger and his organization, winning a $12.5 million verdict that decimated WAR and forced Metzger to make monthly payments to Seraw's estate for twenty years.

JUSTICE FOR THE SERAW FAMILY

Morris Dees holds 9-year-old Henock Seraw in his lap just moments before a jury in Portland, Oregon, returns a $12.5 million verdict against Tom Metzger and the White Aryan Resistance in October 1990. Portland lawyer Elden Rosenthal (right of Dees) assisted in the trial and later joined the SPLC board. Henock, the son of slain Ethiopian student Mulugeta Seraw, was subsequently adopted and raised in California by SPLC board member Jim McElroy, who also assisted Dees with the case. Today, Henock is a pilot for an international airline. Dees and the legal team proved that Metzger and his group were partly responsible for the brutal beating death of Henock's father two years earlier.

At the Pentagon, Weinberger responded to the SPLC's warnings by issuing a directive stating that military personnel must "reject participation in white supremacy, neo-Nazi and other such groups which espouse or attempt to create overt discrimination." The new rule was a good first step, but it didn't go far enough.

Finally, in late 2009, after a series of investigations by the SPLC and appeals to military leaders and Congress, the Pentagon further tightened its policy on extremist activity. Under the new regulations, military personnel "must not actively advocate supremacist doctrine, ideology or causes" or "otherwise advance efforts to deprive individuals of their civil rights." The new rules specified that activities such as recruiting, fundraising, demonstrating or rallying, training, organizing and distributing supremacist material were forbidden. It had taken two decades, but the SPLC's persistence had paid off.

THE SPLC'S LEGAL CAMPAIGN took a heavy toll on the Klan. By the late 1980s, membership had dwindled to an estimated five thousand nationwide, and Klan leaders grew leery of conducting activities that might land them in Dees' line of sight.

Unfortunately, while the Klan was fracturing, the white supremacist movement was morphing into something even more volatile, especially as neo-Nazis and violent, racist skinheads began to appear on the scene. Dees and Cohen realized that these new factions represented a threat as great or greater than the old-line Klan, some of whose leaders were now aligning themselves with the new foot soldiers of the extreme right. One of those leaders was Tom Metzger, a grand dragon of a California Klan group and a prominent former associate of Klan boss David Duke.

In the mid-1980s, Metzger formed a neo-Nazi organization he called the White Aryan Resistance, or WAR. He began publishing a racist and anti-Semitic tabloid that he used to recruit skinheads to be the "shock troops" of the coming revolution. He also established a telephone hotline to disseminate racist information and a bulletin board on a precursor to the Internet to help skinheads communicate with one another. And in 1988, he and his son organized the first-ever hate rock festival, Aryan Fest, in Oklahoma.

That same year, Metzger sent one of his protégés to Portland, Oregon, to organize a skinhead group called East Side White Pride. Three weeks later, a skinhead from that group, Ken Mieske, and two others who had been trained by Metzger's lieutenant, beat to death Ethiopian college student Mulugeta Seraw on the street in Portland. Metzger praised them for doing their "civic duty." Though the skinheads pleaded guilty to murder, Dees believed Metzger also should be held accountable for his role. So, using similar legal doctrines to those he had fashioned for the Michael Donald case and others, Dees filed suit against the Metzgers and WAR.

A Portland jury agreed and awarded $12.5 million in damages to the victim's family.

Metzger, who was personally responsible for $5.5 million of the verdict, lost his house and possessions and was required to make monthly payments to Seraw's estate for twenty years. WAR was crippled, surviving only as a shell of an organization used by Metzger to disseminate his racist propaganda.

More victories followed. A decade later, the SPLC won a $6.3 million verdict against another neo-Nazi group, the Aryan Nations, and its infamous leader, Richard Butler. The suit forced Butler to give up his twenty-acre compound in Hayden Lake, Idaho, which had long been used to host the annual World Aryan Congress of white supremacist leaders.

CONTINUED ON **PAGE 100**

NEO-NAZI PATRIARCH RICHARD BUTLER

Aerospace engineer Richard Butler, a patriarch of the American neo-Nazi movement, in the 1970s established a twenty-acre compound in Hayden Lake, Idaho, that would serve for decades as a headquarters for his group, Aryan Nations, and a haven for violent ex-convicts, racist skinheads and various other racists and anti-Semites. Several of his followers went to prison for plotting to assassinate Morris Dees and bomb the SPLC.

SPLC TAKES DOWN ARYAN NATIONS

Neo-Nazi leader Richard Butler was a minister of Christian Identity, a racist, anti-Semitic theology, and formed the Church of Jesus Christ Christian at his North Idaho compound. In 1999, the SPLC sued Butler after his guards assaulted and shot at a woman and her son who were driving by the Aryan Nations' compound. After a jury in 2000 returned a $6.3 million verdict, Butler was forced to turn his compound over to the plaintiffs. They sold it to a philanthropist, who donated the property—following the demolition of buildings—to a local college.

In 2006, Dees sued another large Klan network, the Imperial Klans of America (IKA), after its members savagely beat Jordan Gruver, a teen of Panamanian-Indian descent, at a county fair in Brandenburg, Kentucky. The IKA served as a networking hub for an array of skinheads, neo-Nazis and Klansmen, and its rural Kentucky compound was the site of the annual Nordic Fest hate rock festival.

At the trial, Dees' co-counsel Bill McMurry elicited testimony that the IKA's leader, Ron Edwards, had been involved in a plot to kill Dees in retaliation for the earlier case against the Aryan Nations. The would-be assassin, Kale Kelly, told jurors that Edwards had given him the rank of lieutenant in a secret cell whose mission was to kill and injure Jews, African Americans and anyone who opposed Edwards. He had handed Kelly a piece of paper with Dees' name on it. After instructing him to assassinate Dees, he burned the paper in a candle's flame.

But the FBI had a secret operative, a former biker named Dave Hall who had infiltrated the Aryan Nations a year earlier and risen quickly through the ranks. Hall, who co-authored the 2008 book *Into the Devil's Den* with his FBI handler, Special Agent Tim Burkey, uncovered the plot at great personal risk. As a result, the FBI arrested Kelly near Cincinnati as he prepared to head south to carry out his plan. He was convicted on weapons charges and served three years in prison.

The SPLC's $2.5 million verdict in 2008 decimated the IKA. At one point, the group boasted of thirty-nine chapters scattered across the country. By 2010, the IKA was reduced to just two, and Edwards was in prison on drug charges. By 2012, the group was defunct.

The SPLC's campaign against white supremacist groups had been extraordinarily successful. It had won crushing civil judgments against ten major white supremacist organizations and fifty individuals who led them or participated in violent acts. It had trained tens of thousands of law enforcement officers and provided vital intelligence to help them combat violent hate groups.

Few doubted the impact of the SPLC's efforts. But perhaps nothing summed it up more than a posting on Stormfront, the largest neo-Nazi Internet forum: *"Galling as it may be, no other single organization has more effectively damaged our Cause."* •

SPLC TAKES ON IMPERIAL KLANS, 2007
Ron Edwards (center) operated one of the largest Klan networks in America, the Imperial Klans of America, which in 2005 had thirty-nine chapters in twenty-six states. His fifteen-acre compound in Dawson Springs, Kentucky, was a hub for white supremacists and the site of Nordic Fest, an annual racist rock festival that brought together violent Klansmen, skinheads and neo-Nazis. The SPLC sued Edwards after his followers brutally beat a minority teen at a county fair in nearby Brandenburg. At the trial, a former Klansman testified that Edwards had once instructed him to kill Morris Dees.

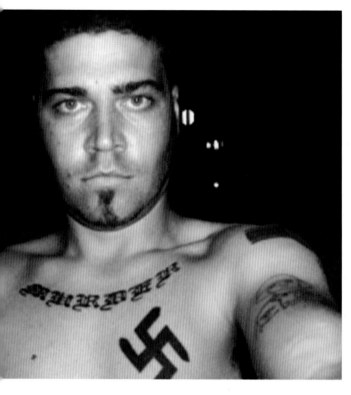  

IMPERIAL KLANS DECIMATED

In its suit against the Imperial Klans of America, the SPLC represented Jordan Gruver, who was 16 and weighed just 120 pounds when he was attacked by four IKA members and savagely beaten at a county fair in 2006. The Klansmen, including Jarred Hensley (far left) and six-foot-nine Andrew Watkins (second from left), called Gruver an "illegal spic" and beat him to the ground, kicking him with steel-toe boots as he curled into a fetal position. Gruver suffered a broken jaw, broken teeth and permanent nerve damage. IKA imperial wizard Ron Edwards (third from left) showed his contempt for the SPLC by tattooing his head prior to a deposition. Morris Dees and the SPLC won a $2.5 million jury award in 2008, effectively ending the IKA.

TRACKING THE MILITIA MOVEMENT

In the 1990s, the SPLC began tracking the rise of the far-right militia movement, based on antigovernment animus and rooted in racist ideologies. Fueling the movement was the 1992 siege at Ruby Ridge, Idaho (left), that left three people dead and the 1993 siege at the Branch Davidian compound (bottom right) in Waco, Texas, where seventy-six people were killed. In 1994, Morris Dees warned Attorney General Janet Reno that the "mixture of armed groups and those who hate" was "a recipe for disaster." Six months later, militia sympathizer Timothy McVeigh bombed the Oklahoma City federal building, killing one hundred and sixty-eight people.

THE HAROLD MANSFIELD CASE

In May 1991, George Loeb murdered 22-year-old Harold Mansfield, a sailor who had served in the Gulf War, in a Mayport, Florida, parking lot. Loeb was a "reverend" in the white supremacist Church of the Creator, which actively encouraged its members to commit violence against Jews and nonwhites—the "mud races"—to help "purify" the white race. Loeb was convicted of murder in July 1992 and sentenced to life in prison. The SPLC sued the Otto, North Carolina-based "church" in 1994, claiming it was also responsible for Mansfield's death. Its newspaper, *Racial Loyalty*, bestowed monthly awards to those who committed racist violence and had honored Loeb for the killing. The SPLC won a $1 million default judgment. But in a sham transaction, the organization transferred its property to neo-Nazi leader William Pierce (above right). The SPLC then won an $85,000 judgment against Pierce, and the proceeds went to Mansfield's mother. Members of the church, which recruited heavily in prisons and conducted paramilitary training for racist skinheads and other white supremacists, also had been responsible for a string of bank robberies and other criminal acts, including the bombing of an NAACP office in Tacoma, Washington.

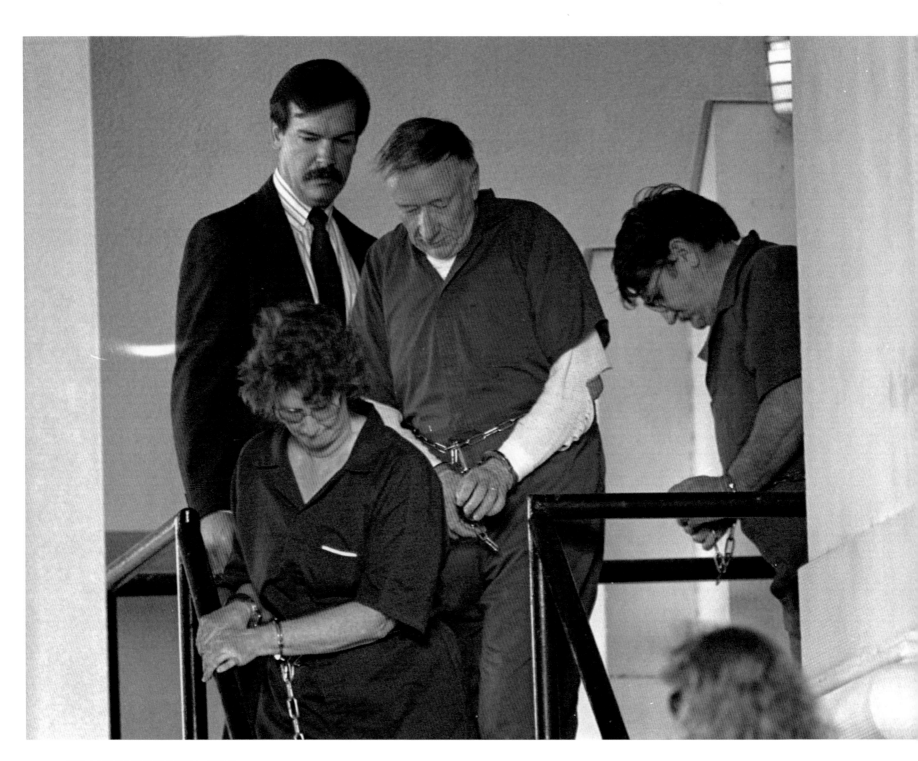

SPLC TARGETED BY EXTREMISTS

Morris Dees and the SPLC have long been targeted by extremists. In November 1995, seven months after the Oklahoma City bombing, the leader of the Oklahoma Constitutional Militia, Willie Ray Lampley, was arrested in a plot to bomb the SPLC and other civil rights organizations. Also arrested that day were his wife, Cecilia Lampley, and John Dare Baird. Kale Kelly (above, left) was part of a conspiracy to assassinate Morris Dees during the Aryan Nations case, but an FBI informant uncovered the plot and Kelly was arrested in April 1999 as he was preparing to track Dees. He served time on related weapons charges. A year earlier, the FBI foiled a plot by the New Order to blow up the SPLC and kill Dees. Violent neo-Nazi Ray Redfeairn (middle, on right), who had earlier shot a police officer in Ohio, was thought to be the architect of the plot. Former prison guard Wallace Weicherding (right) was convicted and sentenced to seventy months in federal prison. He had earlier tried to get into a Dees speech with a .44 Magnum. Several others were imprisoned as well. More than two dozen people have gone to prison in connection with plots to kill Dees or attack the SPLC.

YANKEE
GO
HOME
WWW.SCLOS.ORG

SPLC | NAACP
IN BED
TOGETHER
WWW.SCLOS.ORG

MORRIS DEES
HATES OUR
SOUTHERN
CULTURE
WWW.SCLOS.ORG

PEROUTKA
GOD★FAMILY★REPUBLIC

...UNTIL JUSTICE ROLLS DOWN LIKE WATERS
AND RIGHTEOUSNESS LIKE A MIGHTY STREAM

MARTIN LUTHER KING JR

EXTREMISTS PROTEST SPLC

Far-right extremists have held numerous demonstrations outside the SPLC office in
Montgomery, Alabama, over the years. In 2003, police in riot gear stood watch over
a group of about seventy people that included some of the most prominent leaders of
the American radical right (far left). The white supremacist League of the South, which
advocates Southern secession, waved the Confederate battle flag in front of the Civil Rights
Memorial in 2004 (second from left). Klansmen marched in Montgomery to denounce
Morris Dees (far right) in 1991.

SOUTHERN WHITE KNIGHTS CASE

In 1987, on the anniversary of Dr. Martin Luther King Jr.'s birth, an interracial group marched in Forsyth County, Georgia. But Klansmen showed up and threw rocks and bottles, forcing the marchers back. The SPLC sued the Southern White Knights, the Invisible Empire and a number of individual Klansmen for disrupting the peaceful march. A federal jury awarded nearly $1 million in damages. Some Klan assets were turned over to the NAACP.

THE SPLC'S CAMPAIGN AGAINST NEO-NAZIS

The SPLC has long tracked the neo-Nazi movement in the U.S. and has severely damaged it through litigation and by exposing embarrassing information about its leaders that has caused dissension within groups. By 2008, the National Socialist Movement had become the largest and most prominent neo-Nazi group in the country but was far weaker than its predecessors. Here, the NSM protests immigration in Washington, D.C., on April 19, 2008, the thirteenth anniversary of the Oklahoma City bombing.

THE MACEDONIA BAPTIST CHURCH CASE

One night in June 1995, Klansmen set fire to the Macedonia Baptist Church in Clarendon County, South Carolina, one of several African-American churches burned by arsonists in the mid-1990s. After four men were sentenced to prison for setting the fire that completely destroyed the century-old structure, the SPLC sued the Christian Knights of the Ku Klux Klan, alleging that its leaders encouraged the burning of black churches. At the trial, church board member Jesse Young showed jurors a threat that had been stapled to the church's door. A jury delivered the largest judgment ever against a Klan group—$37.8 million, later reduced by a judge to $21.5 million.

"PATRIOT" RESURGENCE

In 2009, the SPLC documented a powerful resurgence of the antigovernment Patriot, or militia, movement that had been responsible for so much violence in the 1990s, including the Oklahoma City bombing. The key factor: the election of President Obama as the nation's first black president. Over a four-year period, Patriot groups grew from one hundred and forty-nine groups to a peak of thirteen hundred and sixty. Numerous terrorist plots were disrupted by law enforcement.

"PATRIOT" GROUPS 1995–2013

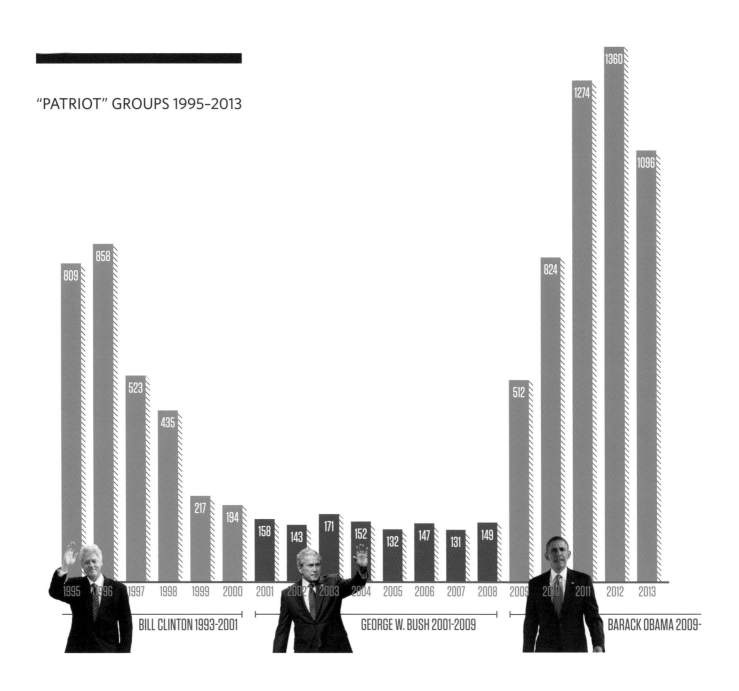

809 | 858 | 523 | 435 | 217 | 194 | 158 | 143 | 171 | 152 | 132 | 147 | 131 | 149 | 512 | 824 | 1274 | 1360 | 1096

1995 | 1996 | 1997 | 1998 | 1999 | 2000 | 2001 | 2002 | 2003 | 2004 | 2005 | 2006 | 2007 | 2008 | 2009 | 2010 | 2011 | 2012 | 2013

BILL CLINTON 1993-2001

GEORGE W. BUSH 2001-2009

BARACK OBAMA 2009-

"SOVEREIGN CITIZENS" RAMPAGE

As part of the far-right "Patriot" movement, so-called sovereign citizens, who claimed they were not subject to most taxes and laws, exploded onto the scene for a second time in the 2000s. At least seven law enforcement officers were killed or wounded in shoot-outs with sovereigns who resisted authority, often during routine traffic stops. On May 20, 2010, 16-year-old Joseph Kane, who was riding with his sovereign father, Jerry Kane, killed two police officers with an assault rifle after the two were stopped on the interstate in West Memphis, Arkansas. Both Kanes were later shot dead by police. The murders were captured by the police car's dashboard camera. Afterward, the local police chief, Bob Paudert, whose son was killed, appeared in an SPLC training video intended to help protect officers from the threat posed by sovereigns. The SPLC distributed more than one hundred thousand videos across the country, free of charge.

NEO-NAZI KILLS SIX AT SIKH TEMPLE
On August 5, 2012, Wade Michael Page walked into the Sikh Temple of Wisconsin in the Milwaukee suburb of Oak Creek and started shooting worshipers with a 9 mm handgun, apparently thinking he was killing Muslims. The temple president, three priests and two others were killed; four people, including a police officer, were wounded. Page shot himself in the head after being wounded by police. The SPLC had a long dossier on Page and quickly alerted the media and the public that Page was a longtime neo-Nazi skinhead and member of a white power rock group.

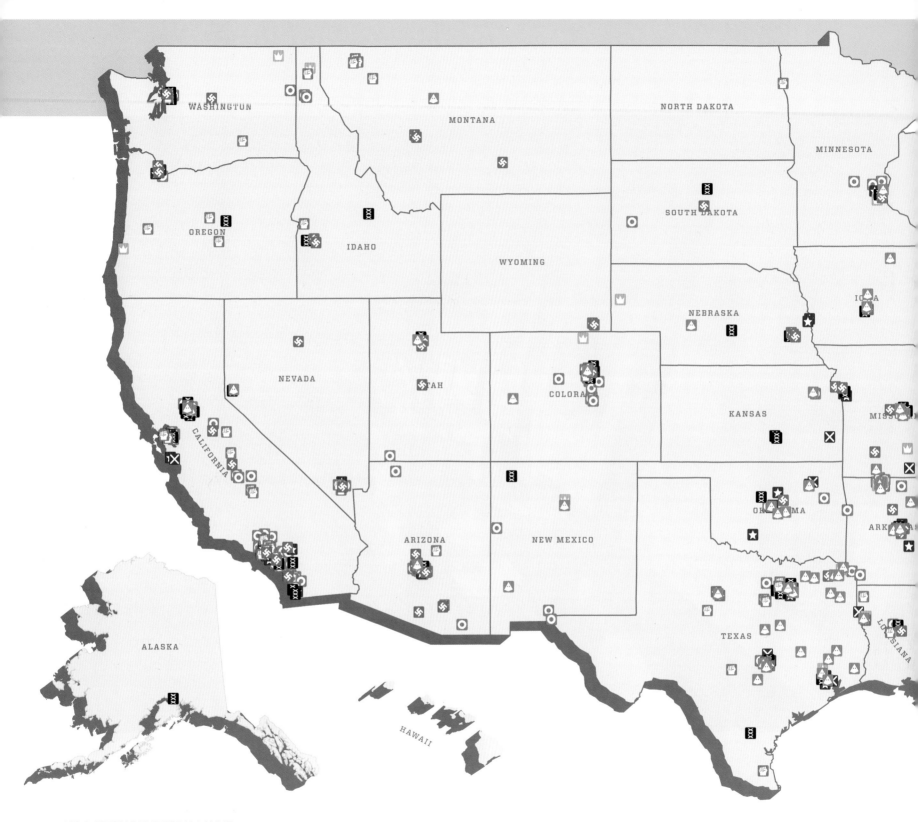

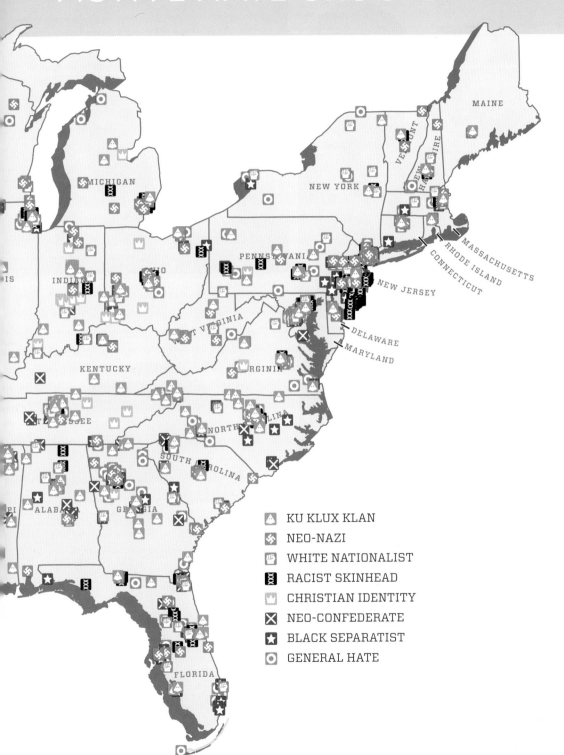

KU KLUX KLAN

NEO-NAZI

WHITE NATIONALIST

RACIST SKINHEAD

CHRISTIAN IDENTITY

NEO-CONFEDERATE

BLACK SEPARATIST

GENERAL HATE

SPLC TRACKS HATE GROUPS

Morris Dees' work fighting the KKK in court led the SPLC to establish a special arm called Klanwatch, later the Intelligence Project as its work expanded to include the tracking of other types of hate groups. In 1990, the SPLC began conducting an annual census of hate groups and plotting their locations on a map, allowing law enforcement, the news media and the public to see where they were operating. Each year, the SPLC releases a report with a new tally of such organizations. Over the decades, the SPLC tracked an inexorable rise in hate groups—to a high of 1,018 in 2011. The annual count helped establish the SPLC as the preeminent authority on radical-right extremists in the U.S.

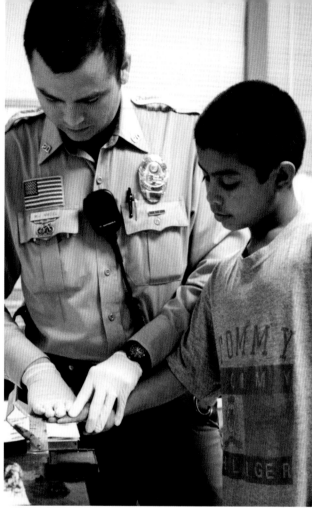

CHAPTER THREE

FIGHTING FOR SOCIETY'S MOST VULNERABLE

AFRICAN AMERICANS WEREN'T THE ONLY ONES who faced systematic discrimination in the early 1970s. A decade after a powerful feminist movement had challenged traditional gender roles in society, women were still viewed paternalistically. In the workplace, especially, inequality was the rule.

Sharron Frontiero found this out firsthand. She was a 23-year-old lieutenant stationed at Maxwell Air Force Base in Montgomery, Alabama. Shortly after getting married, she applied for an increased housing allowance and medical benefits for her husband—perquisites that were automatically granted to married men—because she now had to find off-base housing.

But the Air Force said she wasn't eligible. Unlike men, she had to prove she provided more than half the income for her spouse, a veteran who was attending college under the GI Bill.

Frontiero hoped to find a lawyer who would write a letter demanding her benefits. She found something better—a young lawyer named Joe Levin, who was in the process of transforming his civil rights law partnership with Morris Dees into the nonprofit Southern Poverty Law Center.

"He told me we were dealing with the inequality of law," Frontiero recalled. "The only remedy was a lawsuit that would force a change in the statute."

Levin took the case, and it resulted in a landmark 1973 victory that altered the legal terrain for women

fighting for equal rights. In the first successful gender discrimination case against the federal government, the U.S. Supreme Court ruled 8-1 that the Air Force's policy was unconstitutional.

"There can be no doubt that our Nation has had a long and unfortunate history of sex discrimination," wrote Justice William J. Brennan. "Traditionally, such discrimination was rationalized by an attitude of 'romantic paternalism' which, in practical effect, put women, not on a pedestal, but in a cage." Brennan's opinion represented the first time the Court had applied the due process clause of the Fifth Amendment to enforce equal rights for women.

Later in the decade, as more women headed into the workforce, the SPLC went to court again, this time to challenge a policy in Alabama that denied many women the opportunity to work in law enforcement. A federal lawsuit was brought on behalf of two young women, Dianne Kimberly Rawlinson and Brenda Mieth. Rawlinson had applied to become a counselor with the state's prison system. But despite impressive academic credentials, she was ineligible because she weighed only a hundred and ten pounds—not enough to meet the minimum weight requirement of a hundred and twenty pounds. Likewise, Mieth wanted to be a state trooper but didn't meet the height and weight requirements for that job, which were

CONTINUED ON **PAGE 130**

FRONTIERO SEX DISCRIMINATION CASE
Sharron Frontiero, a young, married Air Force lieutenant stationed in Montgomery, Alabama, was denied housing and spousal medical benefits that were routinely granted to married men. In a landmark 1973 decision, the U.S. Supreme Court ruled the Air Force's policy unconstitutional. Filed by SPLC co-founder Joe Levin, the case became the first successful sex discrimination lawsuit against the federal government and helped pave the way to equal treatment under the law for women.

GENDER BIAS IN LAW ENFORCEMENT, 1976
Dianne Kimberly Rawlinson was 22 when she applied to become a corrections officer in Alabama. She was turned down because she was female, though the official reason was that she weighed only a hundred and ten pounds—ten pounds short of the minimum weight requirement. The SPLC filed a federal sex discrimination suit on behalf of her and another woman, Brenda Mieth, who also didn't meet the state's height and weight requirements to become a state trooper. The case went to the U.S. Supreme Court, which agreed with a lower court's ruling that the state's requirements discriminated against women and had no relationship to the demands of the jobs. Joe Levin met with Rawlinson in 2000.

FIGHTING HOME FORECLOSURES

Viola Hart faced the foreclosure of her home in Eufaula, Alabama, because she stopped paying a contractor after he had performed shoddy plumbing work. She had mortgaged the house to the contractor, who then sold the mortgage to a Florida banking company that, under existing laws, was not responsible for the poor work. The SPLC filed suit on behalf of thirty other poor black families exploited by the same contractor.

THE "BROWN LUNG" CASE, 1979

Nat Wilkins worked at a cotton mill in Opelika, Alabama, for twenty-seven years, inhaling millions of microscopic cotton dust particles that eventually clogged his lungs and made him so ill he could barely work. After filing suit, SPLC lawyers discovered that the company, Westpoint Pepperell, knew that mill workers were in danger of contracting byssinosis, or "brown lung disease," but had concealed that information from its employees. Studies indicated that about 12 percent of mill workers contracted the deadly disease. The case helped clear the way for brown lung victims to receive compensation. By the year 2000, government regulations had virtually eliminated the disease among mill workers.

five-foot-nine and a hundred and sixty pounds. A federal judge ruled in their favor, but the case was appealed to the Supreme Court. In 1977, the Court upheld the ruling, agreeing that the height and weight requirements bore no relationship to the job and discriminated against women.

These were among the first of many important civil rights cases won by the SPLC. Over the next four decades, SPLC lawyers launched dozens of suits on behalf of the powerless or forgotten: prisoners living in barbaric conditions; children abused and neglected in detention and mental health facilities; minorities victimized in hate crimes; gay men and lesbians denied fundamental rights; farmworkers exploited by unscrupulous corporations; immigrants facing racial profiling, discrimination and harassment; and others.

Initially, many of the legal battles were fought for plaintiffs living in Alabama, the heart of Dixie. Even so, the federal court rulings shattered barriers to equality and reverberated throughout the country.

With these cases, many setting historic precedents, the SPLC sought not only justice for individual plaintiffs but systemic reforms that would improve the lives of thousands of other people in similar situations and, ultimately, ensure equality under the law for everyone, regardless of race, ethnicity, gender, sexual orientation, disability, age or socioeconomic status.

WHEN JERRY LEE PUGH ENTERED Alabama's G.K. Fountain Correctional Institute in 1973, he found himself sleeping in a large, massively overcrowded barracks. At night, when there were no guards around, inmates were routinely stabbed, raped and beaten. One night, not long after he arrived, it was his turn. Pugh was beaten so savagely that his attackers, thinking he was dead, stuffed him under his own cot.

Pugh survived and, after months in the hospital where he had a metal plate put in his head, he put his name on an SPLC lawsuit against the state of Alabama, challenging the overcrowding and understaffing that led to so much violence.

The state's four prisons were so overwhelmed that inmates were housed in open barracks, where many slept on the floor, packed tightly into small corridors. There were only half as many guards as needed.

At one prison dormitory, more than two hundred prisoners shared one toilet. Kitchens were unsanitary. Prisoners earned 25 cents each week for their labor and had to use the money to buy essential items like toothpaste, soap and underwear.

In one prison, inmates were sent to a one-man cell called the "doghouse," sometimes for months at a time, for minor infractions. It wasn't uncommon for four or five inmates to be jammed into the doghouse, which had no furniture, no windows, no running water, no lights. Prisoners were fed once a day and given water three times a day. The toilet was a hole in the floor that was flushed once a day from the outside.

Responding to the SPLC's lawsuit, U.S. District Judge Frank M. Johnson Jr.—already famous for striking down Jim Crow laws in Alabama—issued an order that closed the prison doors to new inmates until the state made room for them. He followed that with a historic opinion calling the prisons "wholly unfit for human habitation" and ordering sweeping, highly detailed reforms to remedy conditions that violated the Eighth Amendment's prohibition of "cruel and unusual punishments."

Coming from a longtime nemesis, Johnson's ruling didn't sit well with Alabama Governor George Wallace, with whom the SPLC had earlier clashed over desegregation of the state trooper force. Wallace, who was running in the Democratic primary for president that year, barked that "thugs and federal judges have just about taken over society." He

ALABAMA PRISON CASE, 1974
Prison inmate Jerry Lee Pugh, seen here with Bobby Segall, a private lawyer working in association with the SPLC, was the plaintiff in an SPLC suit challenging the barbaric conditions inside Alabama's dangerously overcrowded prisons. After entering the prison system in 1973, Pugh was assigned to a large, crowded barracks, where violence and rape were common. One night, he was so savagely beaten that his attackers thought he was dead and stuffed him under his cot. U.S. District Judge Frank M. Johnson Jr., who heard the case, was famous for his civil rights rulings, some of them in cases resisted by segregationist Alabama Governor George Wallace.

added that a robust vote for him in the coming election "might give a political barbed wire enema to some federal judges."

But just as Wallace could not stop the integration of public schools years earlier, he could not stop the federal judiciary from compelling the state to clean up its prison system. And after Wallace complained that Johnson was trying to create a hotel atmosphere in the prisons, the judge issued a thundering retort: "I say to you that the elimination of conditions that will permit maggots in a patient's wounds for over a month before his death does not constitute creation of a hotel atmosphere. The elimination of other physical and mental indignities such as the rape of a retarded minor four times in one night, with the prison officials stating to the victim that there was nothing they could do, will not be creating a hotel setting."

Johnson's rejoinder to Wallace was a stark reminder of what was at stake in the SPLC suit. Federal courts would monitor the prison system's progress over the next decade as the SPLC lawyers ensured the reforms Johnson ordered were carried out.

But overcrowding was just one of the problems in the Alabama prison system. In the 1990s, the SPLC worked with private attorneys to seek help for the two thousand mentally ill inmates who were warehoused in Alabama prisons with virtually no treatment. The lead plaintiff was 31-year-old Thomas Bradley, who suffered from schizophrenia and had been undergoing treatment since he was 17.

Bradley's father, writing in a January 1992 court affidavit, described his son's deterioration: "When I saw him in late August, he was incoherent and mumbling, but was able to walk and speak. He was brought to us still wet from a shower and bleeding from being shaved. From that point on, I started requesting and demanding help for him. When I next saw him in late December, I hardly recognized

him. His weight had dropped significantly, to perhaps 110 pounds. He did not seem to recognize me or his mother and did not communicate or show any expression. He was pale and trembling uncontrollably and was in great distress."

Prison officials resisted, but in 1997, a federal magistrate concluded that despite warnings that its system for treating the mentally ill was "fatally flawed," the state had done little to remedy the glaring problems. Seriously ill inmates were locked down in primitive conditions and, if thought suicidal, were stripped and forced to sleep on thin mats. Instead of counseling and therapy, they were simply medicated and banished to isolation cells for long periods— sometimes years.

The case came within days of a federal trial before the Alabama Department of Corrections agreed to a settlement, signed in September 2000, that would result in the opening of a new treatment unit for inmates like Bradley, a 300 percent increase in the number of mental health professionals working in the system, and upgraded psychiatric treatment, therapeutic activities and more.

After twelve years behind bars, Bradley received the help he desperately needed, as did many other long-suffering mentally ill prisoners.

In the meantime, as the Bradley case was winding through the courts, Alabama officials decided to resurrect a relic from the past: chain gangs. Chain gangs were first used in the state following the Civil War. They provided a cheap form of labor and an alternative to rebuilding prisons that had been destroyed. The vast majority of the prisoners on these gangs were African American, and they died at enormously high rates because of the brutality they suffered.

The tactic was abolished throughout the South by the early 1960s amid widespread public revulsion. But in May 1995, Alabama became the first state to reinstate the practice after it was suggested

ALABAMA PRISON CASE
Alabama's four prisons were so overcrowded in the 1970s that many inmates slept on the floor in open barracks or were packed tightly into small corridors. At one dormitory, there was one toilet for more than two hundred prisoners. The case led to a sweeping court order by U.S. District Judge Frank M. Johnson Jr., who called the state's prisons "wholly unfit for human habitation." In 2014, the SPLC again sued the prison system, this time for failing to provide adequate health care.

by Governor Fob James on a talk radio show during the waning days of his gubernatorial campaign the year before. In the new version, inmates wearing leg irons were chained together in groups of five. They were forced to work for ten hours a day picking up litter, breaking rocks, clearing brush and cutting grass with sling blades along the state's highways. One or two rifle-toting guards on horseback typically supervised twenty-five to forty inmates, who wore white uniforms with the words "Chain Gang" emblazoned on their backs. The prisoners, most of whom were assigned to the gangs as punishment for breaking prison rules or violating parole, remained shackled together during meals and roadside toilet breaks. "It wasn't designed for any purpose but to humiliate and degrade," said Michael Austin, who was serving time for a drug charge and ended up on a chain gang. "Just because a person is in prison, he's still a human being. A human being needs to be treated like a human being, not like an animal. If you continue, you'll eventually bring the animal out in them."

Newspapers across the country and the world wrote about the practice that evoked stark images of the state's past, a history stained with racial violence and injustice. "Watching the chain gang at work, it's impossible to wipe away the images of the Old South," wrote a reporter for Florida's *St. Petersburg Times*. "The clinking of chains make an unmistakable music." Later, a report by Amnesty International would single out Alabama for defying international standards banning the use of chains or leg irons. "This is not a deterrent," an Alabama inmate told *The Boston Globe* in 1995. "This is a hatred builder."

Alabama officials, however, delighted in the attention and seemed intent on introducing even more brutal practices into the prison system. "I'd like to have some real electric fence," Ron Jones, Alabama's then-commissioner of corrections, told a European newspaper. "Around five thousand volts. That's what you'd call extremely lethal. I think we should think about caning as well."

Acting as his own attorney, Austin challenged the practice in federal court, but the SPLC soon took up the cause and turned Austin's suit into a class action. The SPLC argued that the "barbarous" practice was intended to do nothing more than degrade and humiliate the prisoners and that it created a serious safety risk to the inmates. For one thing, an accident involving a car could drag the entire gang into it. Inmates also would be virtually defenseless against violence that might break out among other prisoners in the gang as they wielded shovels, sling blades, axes and other metal implements in the merciless Alabama heat for long stretches at a time.

During the course of the lawsuit, SPLC lawyers discovered another sadistic practice that inflicted enormous pain as well as psychological trauma. Inmates who refused or were physically unable to work were handcuffed to a metal bar called the "hitching post," where they were forced to stand in the hot sun all day, sometimes without water or bathroom breaks, their arms raised and bodies contorted.

According to the SPLC's lawsuit, "One chain gang inmate ... was ordered to serve time on the hitching post for refusing to work after he had an epileptic seizure. After being removed from the chain gang and driven back to the prison, the inmate was handcuffed to the hitching post for ten hours. There, the prisoner was forced to stand with his hands above his head for the entire day. His wrists and hands became numb, and he suffered dizziness and constant pain. A disciplinary hearing later cleared him of all charges."

It wasn't long before violence erupted on the chain gangs. One prisoner was shot and killed by a guard as he fought with another inmate. Faced with mounting injuries and fights, the Department of Corrections soon decided to negotiate an end to the SPLC's

CONTINUED ON **PAGE 138**

CHAIN GANG CASE
In 1995, Alabama revived a relic of the Jim Crow-era South: chain gangs. The brutal practice had been abolished throughout the South by the 1960s because of widespread public revulsion. But now, once again, groups of inmates chained together could be seen along Alabama's highways—picking up trash, breaking rocks and wielding sling blades. Faced with mounting injuries and fights, prison officials agreed to halt the practice in a settlement with the SPLC.

THE HITCHING POST

Alabama inmates who disrupted the chain gang or refused to work were handcuffed to a metal bar called the "hitching post" and forced to stand in the hot sun for hours with their arms raised. As part of the SPLC's case against the use of chain gangs, a federal judge in 1996 ruled that the barbaric practice violated the Eighth Amendment. In a separate case, the SPLC represented Larry Hope, seen in these photographs, in his appeal to the U.S. Supreme Court. In that case, the Supreme Court ruled that the hitching post was unconstitutional and that an inmate who suffered injuries while chained to the post had the right to sue for damages.

lawsuit—and the chain gangs. In June 1996, a little more than a year after Governor James had reinstated the practice, it was once again relegated to history.

The hitching post claim went to trial that same year, and a judge ruled that the practice violated the Eighth Amendment's ban on cruel and unusual punishment. Larry Hope, one of the plaintiffs in the case, filed a separate lawsuit for damages. In 2002, the SPLC represented Hope in his case in the U.S. Supreme Court, which ruled that the hitching post was unconstitutional and that an inmate who suffered injuries while chained to the post had the right to sue for damages.

Ensuring humane conditions for prison inmates didn't win the SPLC any popularity contests, particularly in its home state of Alabama. But it affirmed the organization's commitment to justice and its belief that all people—regardless of their status—deserved the protection of the U.S. Constitution.

THE SPLC'S WORK TO UPHOLD the rights of people living in correctional facilities took on new meaning in the following decade as the organization launched a wide-ranging campaign to combat an alarming trend: the increasing emphasis on incarcerating children and teens, many of whom had done nothing more than misbehave in school.

By 2008, an estimated one hundred thousand youths were in custody across the country. The vast majority had not committed violent or serious crimes and did not deserve to be locked up. Many were children like "Darius,"* who was just 9 when he was sent to a detention facility in Alabama. For two months, he languished in a juvenile facility—alone and frightened—before SPLC lawyers won his release and helped him obtain mental health treatment. He missed his tenth birthday party. He missed Thanksgiving. He missed his stepfather's funeral. All because he had "threatened" a teacher with a plastic eating utensil.

Across the country, the headlines rang out with other stories of young children being handcuffed and arrested in school for minor infractions.

The children and teens most at risk of entering this "school-to-prison pipeline" were those who, like Darius, had emotional troubles, learning disabilities or other mental health needs. Some studies suggested that as many as 70 percent of children in juvenile detention facilities had significant mental health or learning disabilities. But rather than receiving the help they needed to succeed in school, these vulnerable youths were being swept into a cold, uncaring maze of lawyers, courts, judges and detention facilities, where they were groomed for a brutal life in adult prisons. Race was a defining factor. African-American youths, typically from low-income families, were locked up at four times the rate of whites. The problem was particularly acute in the Deep South, where the shadow of Jim Crow loomed large and one in four African Americans lived in poverty.

Meanwhile, the adult prison population was booming, primarily as the result of ever-harsher sentences for nonviolent drug offenders. By 2008, the number of prisoners held in state and federal prisons had increased by an astounding 388 percent since 1980—even though the country's total population had grown by just 35 percent. With 1.6 million adults in prison (not counting those in county jails), the United States had not only the highest prison population in the world but also the highest per-capita rate of incarceration. And African-American men were incarcerated at six and a half times the rate of white men.

Now, communities were militarizing their schools and feeding more and more children into the burgeoning corrections system. Police officers patrolled the halls, ready to slap cuffs on unruly children, and school administrators implemented harsh "zero-tolerance" policies that pushed children out of school and funneled them into brutal detention centers.

ATTACKING THE "SCHOOL-TO-PRISON PIPELINE"
In the first decade of the new century, the SPLC launched a broad campaign to reform "zero tolerance" policies that were sending tens of thousands of children from school to detention centers for minor misbehavior. Children, many of them with mental illness and learning disabilities, often languished for weeks or months in these brutal facilities without access to educational, psychological or rehabilitative services.

* Some names have been changed to protect the privacy of SPLC clients.

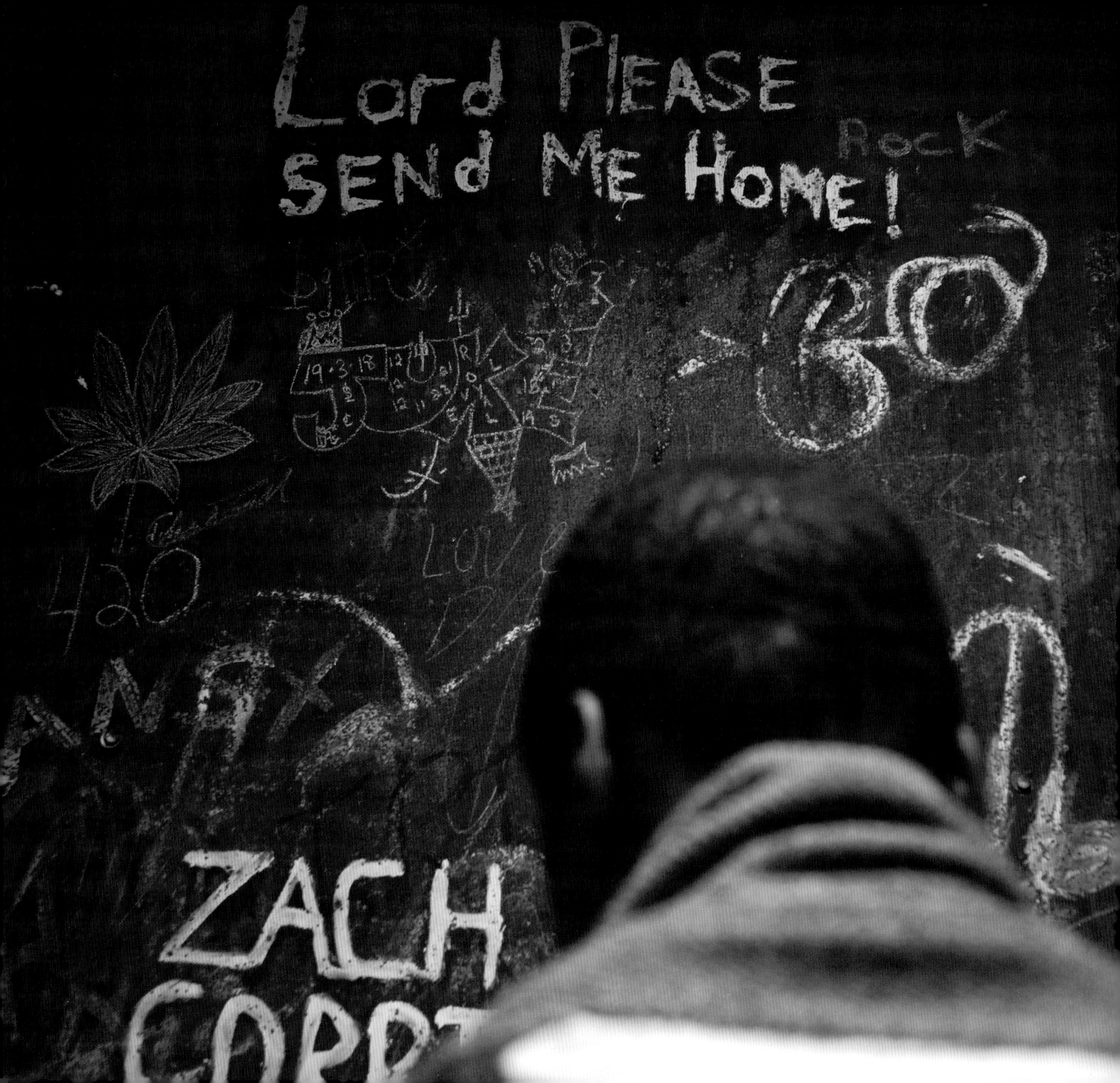
Lord PLEASE
SENd ME HOME!
ROCK
420
ZACH

MISSISSIPPI JUVENILE DETENTION, 2009

A 17-year-old boy, known as "D.W." in an SPLC suit, tried to hang himself with a bed sheet after spending a short time at the Harrison County Juvenile Detention Center in Biloxi, Mississippi, a facility operated by a for-profit company. SPLC lawyers discovered that children at the center, most of whom were simply awaiting court hearings, were living in filthy, shockingly inhumane conditions, spending twenty-three hours a day in their cells without access to adequate medical care. D.W. was forced to sleep on the floor of an overcrowded cell with only a thin, urine-soaked mattress. He also endured a brutal physical assault by guards. Said one child: "I've seen the guards slam kids, mace them and do things they wouldn't even do to their own dog, let alone a human." The SPLC action, one of several targeting abusive juvenile facilities in the Deep South, resulted in broad reforms at the facility.

Faced with this civil rights crisis, the SPLC launched a multifaceted campaign to attack the problem in the Deep South. The organization opened new legal offices in Jackson, Mississippi, Miami and New Orleans to expand its reach and to complement the work of its Alabama staff.

Protecting the rights of children and teens had always been a priority for the SPLC, dating back to Dees' case that integrated the Montgomery YMCA in the early 1970s.

In 1982, the SPLC brought suit against the Bethesda Home for Girls, located in Hattiesburg, Mississippi. Operated by a fundamentalist Baptist minister and his wife, it was part of an interstate network of privately run homes for unmarried teens, many of whom were pregnant. The SPLC's client, 19-year-old "Candy H.," had been persuaded to spend her pregnancy at Bethesda only to find herself held against her will. Candy and dozens of other girls were locked up, denied even the most rudimentary privacy, required to work without compensation, fed little more than fruit and juice, cut off from virtually all communications with their families and the outside world, and beaten for breaking any rules. One expert said the girls were subjected to the kind of mind-control techniques typical of religious cults and Nazi concentration camps. And when some of the girls gave birth, their babies were bartered away to fundamentalist families to help cover the costs of operating the home. Two years earlier, eleven girls had managed to escape, but one was struck and killed by a truck before they were caught and returned to the home. The SPLC's case was settled in 1987 when the minister who owned the home agreed to change many of its practices. But the exposure led to an investigation by Mississippi welfare authorities, resulting in its closure.

In another SPLC-sponsored case, the state of Alabama was forced to halt its practice of sending most orphaned black children to reformatories for juvenile delinquents rather than to state-sponsored foster homes, where white children were sent. In other suits, the SPLC had stopped the state of Michigan from conducting medical experiments on mentally ill children in state hospitals without informed consent; had persuaded a court to strike down a law that allowed Alabama welfare workers to remove a child from an unmarried white woman because she was living with a black man; and had improved the mental health treatment for children in state facilities and foster care.

Many of the SPLC lawsuits brought on behalf of children had a broad impact and improved the lives of many beyond the plaintiffs themselves. But now, the organization's leaders knew that a sustained effort—comprising multiple lawsuits, lobbying efforts, public education, media campaigns and community outreach—was needed to attack the school-to-prison pipeline. The campaign consisted of three major parts. First, the organization would pursue civil rights complaints against schools and school districts that were failing to provide the special education resources that were required by federal law and that could help children with learning disabilities stay in school and out of trouble. Second, it would bring lawsuits to reform harsh disciplinary practices that resulted in children being thrown out of school or into detention. Third, it would file federal lawsuits to stop the shocking abuse and neglect of juveniles held in decrepit detention facilities.

Among the SPLC's clients, most of whom were African American, were a 6-year-old boy who was handcuffed and shackled to a chair by a police officer in a New Orleans school after he argued with another student; a tenth-grader who was expelled in Mississippi for throwing a penny that hit a school bus driver; students in Birmingham, Alabama, who were pepper-sprayed in school by police, sometimes even while restrained, for nonviolent infractions; students in Mobile County, Alabama, who were suspended, without due process, for minor rule violations such as wearing untucked shirts; a student in Jackson, Mississippi, who was handcuffed and shackled to a rail for an entire school day because he wore the wrong color shoes; and a student in Louisiana whose arm was broken by a sheriff's deputy while being detained.

The SPLC's lawyers also exposed grossly inhumane conditions in juvenile detention facilities, where many children landed after being arrested in school.

In Mississippi, the SPLC sued three counties for operating barbaric detention facilities where youths were confined to filthy, overcrowded cells for up to twenty-three hours each day without access to proper educational, medical, mental health or rehabilitative services. Most of them had not even been found guilty of anything but were simply awaiting court hearings. Unlike adults, youths in most cases could not get out on bail while awaiting adjudication. Many

weren't even accused of crimes but were detained for so-called "status" offenses, like truancy, that were "crimes" only because of their age. The vast majority were black.

The facility in the Gulf Coast town of Biloxi, Mississippi, was among the worst. "Toilets and walls are covered with mold, rust and excrement," SPLC lawyers wrote in a federal lawsuit. "Insects have infested the facility, and the smell of human excrement permeates the entire building. Children frequently have to sleep on thin mats that smell of urine and mold. Defendants do not provide children with adequate personal hygiene items."

One SPLC client, a 17-year-old boy known as "D.W." in the suit, was physically abused even while on suicide watch after he had tried to hang himself with a bed sheet. "A guard choked me from behind and slammed me on the floor," he said. "While that guard held me down, another guard dropped his knee in my neck, slammed my face to the floor and then pushed my face into the concrete. I couldn't breathe." Another teen told the SPLC that children were treated like animals. "I've seen the guards slam kids, mace them and do things they wouldn't even do to their own dog, let alone a human."

All of the cases against Mississippi counties resulted in settlement agreements that required officials to transform the facilities to protect the rights and well-being of detained children. But the SPLC also was forced to sue the state of Mississippi over the conditions at two prisons for youthful offenders.

In one case, the state decided to close its notorious Columbia Training School seven months after the SPLC filed suit in federal court to stop what the lawsuit called "horrendous" physical and sexual abuse of teenage girls and to ensure they were getting mental health and rehabilitative treatment. The SPLC represented six girls ranging in age from 13 to 17; all suffered from mental illness and all had been sent to

COLUMBIA TRAINING SCHOOL CASE, 2007

Teenage girls at the Columbia Training School, a prison for girls in Jackson, Mississippi, were subjected to horrendous physical and sexual abuse. The SPLC filed suit on behalf of six girls, all of whom suffered from mental illness and were committed for nonviolent offenses. Five of the girls had been shackled for twelve hours each day for periods ranging up to a month as punishment for unproven allegations that they planned to escape. Three of the girls cut themselves while on suicide watch, during which time they received no psychological help. While in an isolation cell for fourteen hours, one girl carved the words "HATE ME" into her forearm. Seven months after the SPLC lawsuit exposed the brutal conditions at the prison, the state decided to close the facility and announced it would seek to incarcerate fewer juveniles and provide better services for at-risk children.

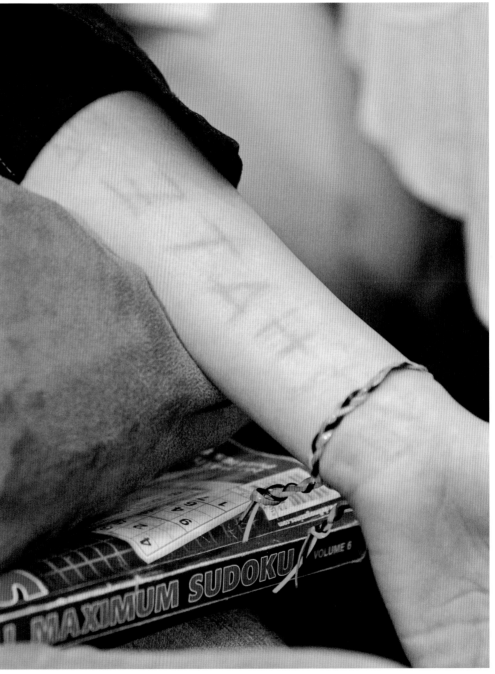

Columbia for nonviolent offenses. Five of the girls had been shackled for twelve hours a day, some for as long as a month, as punishment for unsubstantiated allegations of an escape plot. One had been sexually assaulted by a guard while confined to a segregated area. Several had been placed in isolation for long periods, without treatment, after trying to kill themselves.

Another SPLC case resulted in the removal of teenage boys, some as young as 13, from the Walnut Grove Youth Correctional Facility, a privately operated prison near Jackson. The suit ended with a sweeping consent decree designed to end the inhumane and unconstitutional conditions there—conditions worsened by the cost-cutting of a for-profit corporation that operated the prison under contract with the state.

Among the inmates there was "David" (not his real name). In 2010, his father arrived for a visit only to be told David wasn't there. Remarkably, the prison system didn't seem to know where his son was—or wouldn't tell him. After a frantic search, he found David, who had just turned 21, at a hospital in a town located hours away from the prison. David could barely move, let alone sit up. He couldn't see or talk or use his right arm. "He's got this baseball-size knot on the back of his head," his father said. "He's got cuts all over him, bruises. He has stab wounds. The teeth in the front are broken. He's scared out of his mind. He doesn't have a clue where he's at—or why."

Though he had found his son, David's father still had no answers. No one would tell him what had happened—that is, until he received a phone call from an SPLC advocate who was investigating Walnut Grove. "When I was at my wit's end and couldn't get anywhere, an advocate from the SPLC actually found me. She said, 'Your son was in a riot.' They [SPLC lawyers] just took bits [of information] and started putting this puzzle together. Without them, we wouldn't have a leg to stand on."

David had suffered severe brain damage. A U.S. Department of Justice report about the conditions at Walnut Grove later noted that after weeks of hospitalization, his "previously normal cognition resembled that of a two year old."

In the dry language typical of such reports, the DOJ investigators wrote that on February 27, 2010, "a youth melee resulted in the stabbing of several youth. ... One of the injured youth ... suffered irreparable brain damage and sustained a fractured nose, cuts and stab wounds." Others were stabbed, punched, kicked, stomped and thrown from an upper floor to a lower one. David and his cellmate, who was stabbed in the head, were both nearly killed. A dozen were hospitalized.

There was another shocking detail: A female guard had "endorsed the disturbance by allowing inmates into an authorized cell to fight," the DOJ report said. She was fired but not charged with any crime. The guard's involvement, it turned out, wasn't uncommon. Investigations showed that guards frequently instigated or incited youth-on-youth violence. Often, they were the perpetrators.

What happened to David was symptomatic of a for-profit youth prison that was completely out of control. The SPLC's investigation, begun in 2006, turned into a federal lawsuit. And on March 26, 2012, U.S. District Judge Carlton W. Reeves issued a blistering court order approving a settlement that demanded reforms. He wrote that GEO Group Inc., the company that ran Walnut Grove, had "allowed a cesspool of unconstitutional and inhuman acts and conditions to germinate."

Violence by youths and guards wasn't the only problem. Neither were the gang affiliations of some guards. Or the grossly inadequate medical and mental health care. Or the proliferation of drugs and other contraband. Or the lack of educational and rehabilitative programs. Or the wild overuse of pepper spray

WALNUT GROVE PRISON CASE, 2010
Michael McIntosh testifies before a Mississippi House committee about the pervasive violence, grossly deficient medical care, and other dangerous conditions his son endured at the Walnut Grove Youth Correctional Facility, which was operated by a private, for-profit company. McIntosh's son (above) suffered brain damage and other severe injuries during a melee that the U.S. Justice Department concluded was facilitated by a guard. In a settlement with the SPLC, the state agreed to remove youths from the prison and provide them with an array of rehabilitative services and stronger protections from sexual abuse and violence.

on passive youths. Indeed, the DOJ found that sexual abuse—including brutal youth-on-youth rapes and "brazen" sexual misconduct by prison staffers who coerced youths—was "among the worst that we have seen in any facility anywhere in the nation." What's more, both the prison staff and the Mississippi Department of Corrections, which paid GEO $14 million each year to run the prison, showed "deliberate indifference" to these problems. In other words, nobody cared. The bottom line—private profit, secured in part by dangerously understaffing the prison—was more important than providing humane conditions and services that would protect boys and young men from violence and help get them back on the right track.

For the youths at Walnut Grove, the settlement agreement offered hope. And it represented a sea change in the way Mississippi treated children in its custody. The state was required to remove all boys under 18 and certain others from the prison and house them in separate juvenile facilities. Pepper spray could no longer be used as punishment. Guards were no longer allowed to rely on prisoners to enforce rules or punish others. Youths could not be subjected to solitary confinement. Regular rehabilitative, educational and recreational programs would be available. Mental health and medical care would be required. And, "at all times," youths would be provided with "reasonably safe living conditions and will be protected from violence" and sexual abuse.

Meanwhile, GEO, the country's second largest prison company, decided to cancel its $21 million-a-year contract to operate a separate prison in Mississippi. The state then cut ties with the company, ending its involvement in the Mississippi prison system.

Litigation wasn't the only tool employed by the SPLC to reform the juvenile justice system. In Mississippi, the organization championed legislation to keep children out of detention and expand the use of alternative measures that left them in their own communities. These measures reduced the number of incarcerated children in the state by 90 percent.

In Alabama, a state where eight in ten incarcerated children were locked up for nonviolent misbehavior, the SPLC's work also produced remarkable results. There, rather than pursue a litigation strategy, the organization in 2005 began working quietly behind the scenes with local communities and top-level officials in all three branches of government, including a Republican governor and a Democratic chief justice, to enact changes that would revolutionize the state's approach to juvenile justice and school discipline. Not only did the SPLC work with the court system to enact administrative changes that helped children, its expert on the state's policies drafted landmark legislation and then helped push it through a conservative legislature. Among other reforms, sentencing rules were rewritten so that "status" offenders were no longer sent to detention. The results were stark: By 2011, the number of children in custody had dropped by 60 percent. And the money allocated to "community-based alternatives" to incarceration had risen by nearly 600 percent.

The SPLC's efforts to attack Alabama's school-to-prison pipeline were paying off as well. In Birmingham, the state's largest city, five hundred students each year were being arrested and sent into the juvenile justice system. Those arrests were reduced by more than 70 percent after the SPLC intervened. In Jefferson County, where Birmingham is located, commitments to juvenile detention were reduced from more than seven hundred annually to just two hundred. Suddenly, a state not known for its leadership on social issues, was seen as a model for reform efforts across the country—a status due in large part to the work of the SPLC.

CONTINUED ON **PAGE 151**

REFORMING JUVENILE JUSTICE
The SPLC's campaign to reform harsh juvenile justice and school discipline policies helped usher in broad changes in several Deep South states through a combination of litigation, legislative advocacy and public education. In Mississippi, for example, the number of incarcerated children fell by 90 percent. In Alabama, the number in custody dropped by 60 percent, and children were no longer locked up for noncriminal offenses such as truancy.

HELPING CHILDREN WITH DISABILITIES

The SPLC has long championed the rights of children, particularly those with disabilities. Six-year-old Danielle Brown was born with a severe speech disorder that left her without the ability to form sounds to make words. She could understand what people were saying to her—particularly when she was taunted at school—but she needed a special device that used symbols, pictures and a keyboard to help her communicate. The Medicaid agency, however, refused to pay for it. The SPLC filed suit in 1998, resulting in a settlement in which the agency agreed to begin paying for the device for the children who needed it, estimated at thirty-five each year. "This will open up a door for her," said her mother. "She will now be limited only by her imagination."

By the time Joe Bates (with his mother, Carolyn) finished middle school in 2004, he had fallen years behind his classmates. But school officials in Selma, Alabama, claimed he was cured of his learning disabilities and refused to provide the special services he needed. After the SPLC filed a federal lawsuit, the school system agreed to accommodate Bates' needs. The change in his academic achievement was remarkable. "My child went from a non-reader to an advanced placement student making all As," said his mother, after her son graduated from high school and was accepted into a community college. "If not for the SPLC's help, my child would not have reached his full potential, and he never would have been admitted to any college."

ACCESS TO COLLEGE FOR IMMIGRANT CHILDREN

Wendy Ruiz was a U.S. citizen who was born in Miami and spent her entire life in Florida. But when she was ready for college, she was classified as an out-of-state student—nearly tripling her tuition costs and putting college out of reach—because her parents were undocumented immigrants. The SPLC filed suit in 2011, and a federal judge struck down Florida's discriminatory policy. Joel Licea, also a U.S. citizen, faced the same situation in South Carolina, where he was born and raised. Co-captain of his high school soccer team, student body president, and one of the top students in his class, he dreamed of becoming the first in his family to attend college. Using the precedent set in the Florida case, the SPLC intervened on his behalf and persuaded the University of South Carolina to reverse its policy. Many other students across the Deep South were helped by the SPLC's campaign to guarantee access to education for the children of immigrants.

VIETNAMESE FISHERMEN CASE, 1981

In one of the SPLC's first cases against the Klan, Morris Dees sued Louis Beam and his Texas Knights of the Ku Klux Klan for launching a campaign of terror against Vietnamese shrimpers who were operating in Galveston Bay, Texas. The Vietnamese refugees had settled in the Seabrook community after being forced to flee their country following the fall of Saigon in 1975. Beam was a volatile, violent man—a former helicopter door gunner in the Vietnam War, an associate of America's most prominent neo-Nazi, Richard Butler, and the "grand dragon" of his own paramilitary-style Klan group. In 1981, just before the shrimping season opened, rifle-toting Klansmen cruised the bay in a trawler equipped with a small cannon and an effigy hung from the riggings.

In other states, similar changes were taking place. In Louisiana's Jefferson Parish, where the SPLC had filed a federal civil rights complaint over the school district's treatment of children with learning disabilities, the number of those children who were removed from school for more than ten days plunged by 90 percent. In Palm Beach County, Florida, a similar SPLC complaint led to an important settlement with the nation's eleventh largest school district in a state where schools sent nearly twenty-seven thousand children into the juvenile justice system during the 2004-2005 school year, typically for schoolyard brawls and other minor offenses.

By 2014, much work remained, but it was clear that the SPLC's strategy was paying great dividends. Thousands of vulnerable children had been kept in school and out of juvenile court. States in the Deep South were reforming Jim Crow-era justice systems that did more to criminalize children—particularly black youths and those with learning disabilities—than to help them lead productive lives. And some of the nation's most brutal juvenile prisons and detention centers had been either closed or transformed.

IN THE SPRING OF 1981, a dangerous confrontation was brewing on Galveston Bay in Texas.

Several years earlier, Vietnamese refugees had settled in the fishing community of Seabrook after fleeing their country in the aftermath of the Vietnam War. To make a living, these men and women—U.S. allies during the war—had acquired shrimp trawlers. But the local white fishermen, many of them descended from generations of watermen, did not welcome them with open arms.

Now, tempers were reaching a boiling point.

In an attempt to drive out the Vietnamese shrimpers, some of the locals sought out an emerging Klan leader named Louis Beam, a former Vietnam War helicopter door gunner. Beam, who had established the Texas Knights of the Ku Klux Klan and a heavily armed paramilitary wing he called the Texas Emergency Reserve, was training his growing legion of racist followers in guerrilla tactics for what he believed was a looming "race war."

The "grand dragon," as he called himself, was a dangerous, violent man who was rising quickly through the ranks of the white supremacist movement and who would become one of its principal theorists and strategists. After returning from Vietnam in 1968, full of rage against communists, he had joined the Alabama-based United Klans of America, the group responsible for some of the most heinous violence of the civil rights movement, and later became a follower of America's most prominent neo-Nazi, Richard Butler. He also had a history of run-ins with the law. In the early 1970s, Beam was accused of bombing a left-wing radio station in Houston and of firing a gun into local Communist Party headquarters but was never tried for those crimes.

With a new enemy to fight, one that he conflated with the Viet Cong soldiers he fought in Southeast Asia, Beam wasted little time unleashing a campaign of terror on Galveston Bay.

"It's going to be a hell of a lot more violent than it was in Korea or Vietnam," Beam told a mob of cheering fishermen at a rally during which a boat adorned with the name "USS Vietcong" was burned. "If you want our country for the whites, you're going to have to get it the way our founding fathers got it—with blood, blood, blood." Beam then offered to train the fishermen at his paramilitary camps. "When you come out of there, you'll be ready for the Vietnamese."

From there, the intimidation quickly escalated. In the following weeks, Klansmen burned crosses in the yards of Vietnamese fishermen. A Vietnamese boat

CONTINUED ON **PAGE 154**

THE SPLC SHUTS DOWN TEXAS KLAN GROUP

The Vietnamese community on Galveston Bay was terrified by the Klan's intimidation tactics. Weapons were brandished, crosses were burned, and several fishing vessels were torched by Klansmen seeking to drive out the immigrants. Klan leader Louis Beam—earlier accused of bombing a left-wing radio station in Houston— seemed to relish the prospect of bloodshed, telling white fishermen that the fight would be "a hell of lot more violent than it was in Korea or Vietnam." But despite being threatened by Beam, Morris Dees and the SPLC obtained a court order that stopped the campaign of terror and shut down his paramilitary training bases. It was the first of many victories won by the SPLC on behalf of vulnerable immigrants, and for the Klan, the first of many legal setbacks at the hands of SPLC lawyers.

was burned, as several others had been earlier. Vietnamese fishermen and Americans who cooperated with them were threatened, sometimes with weapons.

Then, in a particularly menacing display two months before the opening of shrimp season, robed Klansmen armed with shotguns and assault rifles cruised the bay in a trawler equipped with a small cannon and a human figure hanging in effigy from the rigging. The Klansmen docked near the home of one of the leaders of the Vietnamese fisherman and terrorized his family.

The Vietnamese community was terrified.

Morris Dees, who was embroiled in a court fight with the Klan in Alabama, had earlier caught wind of the volatile situation in Texas. All of a sudden, after a brief period of dormancy, the Klan appeared to be re-emerging across the country as new, militant leaders like Beam capitalized on a political shift to the right to recruit members into what was becoming a revolutionary movement, as opposed to earlier Klan operations that had sought to maintain the status quo of Jim Crow segregation.

After reading about the Klan's boat ride in *The New York Times*, Dees decided to pay a visit to Col. Nguyen Van Nam, one of the leaders of the Vietnamese community in Seabrook. A former Army commander, Nam had fled his country after the fall of Saigon in 1975 with the knowledge that staying would mean death or prison at the hands of the country's new Communist rulers. He was proud to be living in America, telling Dees he had battled the North Vietnamese until the last Americans were safely evacuated. "And now this Louis Beam say we are Communists," he said.

Dees relished the idea of taking on Beam. The Vietnamese were reluctant, however, fearing retaliation if Dees—"demon Dees," in Beam's words—went to court on their behalf. Many of the fishermen had already put their boats up for sale.

But Dees persuaded them to move forward. With shrimp season approaching, he and his colleagues filed suit in federal court. Over the ensuing weeks, Dees and his legal team endured numerous threats from Beam, who at one point brought a concealed pistol to a deposition.

The intimidation tactics continued, aimed at both the SPLC legal team and the Vietnamese. At one point, the group's elders decided to abandon the suit. But Dees argued passionately against the retrenchment, explaining the history of the Klan and its terrorism during the civil rights movement. "It may be the fishermen that feel the heat now, but you can be sure that if they get the fishermen to give up today, then they'll go after the rest of you tomorrow. 'Why should the Seven-Eleven be run by a foreigner? Why aren't there any Americans employed at the flower shop? This is hurting American business.' That's what they'll say. You have just as much right to be here as Louis Beam. That's what America is all about."

Armed with video footage of Beam's paramilitary camps and other evidence, Dees won an injunction barring Beam and his Klan thugs from engaging in violence or acts of intimidation against the Vietnamese. Beam also was ordered to shut down his paramilitary force, which violated Texas law.

The victory meant the Vietnamese could earn their living in peace. For the Klan, it was among the first of many setbacks at the hands of Dees and the SPLC, setting the stage for numerous criminal plots to exact revenge in the years ahead.

For the SPLC, it marked the first of many cases filed to protect the rights of immigrants.

More than two decades later, Dees and the organization began to see another form of discrimination: the rampant exploitation of migrant workers and foreign laborers, mostly from Latin America, who were lured to the United States to fill low-wage jobs in America's fields and factories.

HURRICANE KATRINA CLEANUP CASE, 2006
In the wake of Hurricane Katrina, the SPLC filed lawsuits against several large contractors that exploited vulnerable migrant workers and illegally withheld wages they had earned while performing grueling work to remove debris and rebuild New Orleans. In one case, a lawsuit led to an agreement with Belfor USA Group to pay overtime wages that had been illegally withheld. The exploitation was part of a broader pattern of abuse by companies using migrant labor.

GUEST WORKER FORESTRY CASES, 2005

Beginning in 2005, the SPLC launched a series of lawsuits on behalf of foreign guest workers who were lured to the United States only to be systematically abused by large forestry companies operating in the South's timberlands. The SPLC uncovered shocking human rights abuses in a system that seemed designed to exploit the world's poorest, most desperate workers to pad the profits of unscrupulous employers. Through its suits, the SPLC recovered millions of dollars in stolen wages and spurred major reforms.

As a boy, Dees had worked long days alongside the farmhands in the hot, dusty cotton fields of his father's small farm in Alabama. He knew the meaning of grueling work and was outraged to discover that large, wealthy corporations were ruthlessly abusing workers at the lowest rungs of the social and economic ladder.

They were workers like Hernan. Desperate for work in his hometown in Mexico, he had agreed to become a "guest worker" in the United States. While the opportunity looked good on paper, Hernan didn't realize the guest worker program was, in the words of former House Ways and Means Committee Chairman Charlie Rangel, the "closest thing to slavery I've ever seen."

Hernan signed up to work as a tree planter for a forestry company in Arkansas but instead was transported to Louisiana and put to work on a sweet potato farm. He and the other Mexican workers slept in an abandoned house with no door and no glass, except for a few broken shards, in the windows. There was no electricity and no heat. There were a few mattresses but no blankets. When it rained at night, the men huddled in corners to escape the water leaking through the roof.

In violation of federal law, their employers based the workers' pay on how many buckets of potatoes they filled, not how many hours they worked. "The first week we were not paid," Hernan said. "The second week we were paid $70. We had been working every day from 5 a.m. to 5 p.m., with 30 minutes for lunch."

Eventually, the men fled from the farm but without their passports, which had been held hostage by the contractor who imported them. After the men left, their wives in Mexico received calls from the contractor saying they had to each pay him $2,000 or their husbands would be reported to immigration authorities or incarcerated in the United States.

Conditions were no better for thousands of forestry workers lured from Latin America. Desperate Guatemalan men from the impoverished region of Huehuetenango paid an average of $2,000 each in recruiting fees and travel costs to obtain seasonal jobs planting pines in the Southeast. Many borrowed the money at exorbitant rates, leaving them deeply in debt and vulnerable to exploitation by their employers. Most were required to leave some form of collateral, generally a property deed, with an agent in Guatemala to ensure they would "comply" with the terms of their contract. This meant there was little chance they would complain about being illegally underpaid.

"Our pay would come out to approximately $25 for a 12-hour workday," said Escolastico De Leon-Granados, a Guatemalan who became an SPLC client.

Added Alvaro Hernandez-Lopez, "What I earned planting trees in the States was hardly enough to pay my debts. It was really hard for us to fight to get to the States legally and then not earn any money."

Another worker, Armenio Pablo-Calmo, said that sometimes he and others would spend a whole day clearing brush to make room to plant seedlings. "We were not paid at all for [this work]. We also never received overtime pay, despite the fact that we worked much more than forty hours per week."

In 2005, the SPLC began filing a series of class action lawsuits against major forestry companies operating in the national forests and large private timber tracts across the Southeast. As the SPLC lawyers delved deeper, they uncovered shocking human rights abuses in a system that seemed designed to exploit the poorest, most desperate workers in the world to pad the profits of unscrupulous employers.

The abuse was occurring in other industries, as well.

Along the Gulf Coast, hundreds of skilled workers from India had each paid more than $10,000 to work in shipyards after being falsely promised the opportunity to live permanently in the United States. To raise the money, one worker represented by the SPLC, Josy, put up his family's land and home as collateral, borrowed money and pawned heirloom jewelry. He quickly found out that the recruiting pitches had been illusory. For one thing, as a guest worker, there was no hope of permanent residency.

"When I arrived at the labor camp, I was horrified and stunned to see the living conditions," Josy said. "Twenty-four men slept in one room with bunk beds. There were only four showers, two toilets and two sinks. The space was incredibly cramped, and there was very little room to walk." Guards were stationed at the gates of the isolated labor camp, and no visitors were allowed. "I felt like we were living in a jail." When workers complained about the conditions, the company sent in guards before dawn one morning to "arrest" and deport workers who were organizing protests.

STANDING UP FOR MIGRANT WORKERS

The SPLC filed numerous lawsuits to stop the exploitation of farm workers and other migrants who labored in the fields and factories to put food on the country's tables but subsisted at the margins of society. Women working in agriculture and food-processing faced particular hardships, often enduring sexual harassment and violence on the job. Many wore bandanas to hide their faces in an effort to ward off sexual attention. The SPLC exposed the harsh conditions they faced—often in silence, unable to speak out about the indignities they suffered and the crimes committed against them.

To Dees, the treatment of guest workers was a human rights crisis, but one largely hidden from the view of Americans who benefited from the labor but knew nothing of the abuses. Not only was this system anathema to American ideals of justice, it was harmful to low-wage U.S. workers. With access to a steady stream of highly vulnerable, impoverished foreign laborers who had little or no way to stand up for their rights, employers had little incentive to hire U.S. workers who demanded fair pay and decent working conditions.

The SPLC mounted a broad assault against the injustices they discovered in the guest worker program, bringing case after case against abusive employers and recovering more than $20 million on behalf of exploited workers. Many of the cases also established legal precedents and prompted headlines across the country, putting other employers on notice that they could be held accountable for taking advantage of their "guests."

As the SPLC worked to protect the rights of guest workers, the country was being riven by a fierce debate over the rising number of Latino immigrants streaming across the border in search of jobs and a better life. By 2006, as many as 12 million unauthorized immigrants were living in the country, many of them working in an underground economy. Nativist sentiments were rising, and violent hate crimes against Latinos were becoming increasingly common. There had been a 35 percent increase in just three years.

In the border states, far-right extremists began to form paramilitary-style vigilante groups, like the Minuteman Project, to patrol the border with Mexico and harass immigrants. One of the earliest, Ranch Rescue, boasted 250 volunteers, many of them former police officers and mercenaries, and was celebrated for its efforts in *Soldier of Fortune* magazine.

In 2003, a Texas ranch owner invited Ranch Rescue to set up a base of operations on his land so it could launch armed patrols to search for unauthorized immigrants crossing the border. Members wore camouflage fatigues and were equipped with high-powered rifles, handguns, night-vision goggles, machetes, two-way radios, all-terrain vehicles and a Rottweiler trained to track humans. One day in March, they spotted what they were looking for—a Salvadoran couple crossing the desert. Ranch Rescue leader Jack Foote later claimed that "[t]hese two trespassers were treated with the utmost of kindness and respect."

But that isn't what happened at all. Instead, Fatima Leiva and Edwin Mancia were terrorized by the vigilantes. After a brief chase, they were captured and forced to the ground. Mancia was struck on the head with a pistol and attacked by the Rottweiler. Held at gunpoint, the two were interrogated, accused of being drug smugglers and threatened with death. After being illegally detained for more than an hour, the traumatized immigrants were released.

Two of the men were charged with crimes. But Dees knew that more needed to be done to stop the escalation of violence by these brazen vigilantes. So, teaming with the Mexican American Legal Defense and Educational Fund and several Texas lawyers, the SPLC filed suit. "If these groups and the ranchers who conspire with them have to pay through their pockets, they will think twice before attacking peaceful migrants," Dees said.

The suit netted nearly $1.5 million in judgments and settlements against the rancher and two Ranch Rescue members, including Foote, who had described Mexicans as "dog turds." The other member, Casey Nethercott, was forced to turn over his seventy-acre Arizona ranch, used as a headquarters and paramilitary training ground, to the plaintiffs. "It is poetic justice that these [migrant] workers now own this

RANCH RESCUE CASE, 2003

As the debate over Latino immigration heated up, far-right extremists began forming armed vigilante groups to patrol the Mexican border. Members of one such group, Ranch Rescue, assaulted and terrorized Salvadorans Fatima Leiva and Edwin Mancia as they were crossing the desert in Texas. An SPLC lawsuit on the couple's behalf netted nearly $1.5 million in judgments and settlements against group members and a rancher who had invited Ranch Rescue to set up a base of operations on his land. One of the Ranch Rescue leaders, Casey Nethercott (middle) was forced to turn over his seventy-acre ranch in Arizona—which was being converted into a paramilitary training ground for the group—to the Salvadorans to satisfy his portion of the judgment. He also was sentenced to five years in prison for weapons charges in connection with the assault.

land," said Dees, who noted the group bore many similarities to the hate groups he had sued earlier. "This sends a strong and important message to those who come to the border to use violence."

The SPLC worked not only in courts of law, but in the court of public opinion.

Racist propaganda about Latinos, often originating in hate groups, was finding its way into the mainstream news media and being increasingly parroted by right-wing politicians. SPLC investigators worked diligently to root out these falsehoods and trace them to their source.

In one high-profile example, the organization became embroiled in a highly public spat with CNN anchor Lou Dobbs, who had taken to bashing Latino immigrants virtually every day on his show and was providing a public platform for white supremacist sympathizers. In 2007, a correspondent on his show reported an especially inflammatory falsehood: the claim that seven thousand new cases of leprosy had appeared in the United States in a recent three-year period, due in large part to immigrants. The real number of cases was about four hundred, and there was no evidence whatsoever to link those cases to immigrants. But Dobbs insisted he was right, famously telling Lesley Stahl of 60 Minutes, "If we reported it, it's a fact."

In Dobbs' unbridled vilification of Latinos, Dees saw echoes of the rhetoric employed by people like George Wallace during the civil rights era, when white supremacists waged a campaign of bombings and murders in a vain attempt to intimidate the African-American community and stop the civil rights movement. "This kind of racist demagoguery not only encourages violence but justifies it to those who believe their way of life is under attack," Dees said.

Representatives from the SPLC appeared on Dobbs' show to set the record straight, but Dobbs was unrepentant.

The controversy raged for years. Other media figures began to investigate Dobbs' claims. *The New York Times* columnist David Leonhardt, using the SPLC as his main source, concluded that Dobbs' claim about leprosy cases had no basis in fact and that he had a "somewhat flexible relationship with reality."

The SPLC's campaign to make Dobbs tell the truth gained steam as Dobbs found himself increasingly under attack and CNN executives felt the pressure to rein in the host, who seemed to be veering further into extremist territory.

Finally, Dobbs went too far, even for the executives who had continued to support him publicly.

In July 2009, SPLC President Richard Cohen publicly called for CNN to fire Dobbs after the anchor joined with the discredited "birther" movement by questioning the authenticity of President Obama's birth certificate. In a letter to CNN, Cohen noted that Dobbs had made a number of false claims about immigrants, including the assertion that "illegal aliens" filled one-third of U.S. prison and jail cells. "Respectable news organizations should not employ reporters willing to peddle racist conspiracy theories and false propaganda," Cohen wrote.

Within four months, Dobbs was off the air.

It was an important victory but only one facet of the SPLC's broader battle for human dignity.

Across the country, immigrants were not only suffering from hate crimes but discrimination and human rights violations as well. The story of Cirila Baltazar-Cruz and her baby girl was a prime example.

Cirila gave birth at a hospital in Pascagoula, Mississippi, in November 2008. Two days later, state welfare workers took the child away amid false allegations leveled by a hospital employee. Cirila, a Mexican immigrant, could not defend herself because she spoke no English and barely any Spanish, but rather an indigenous language. Her baby girl was

CONTINUED ON **PAGE 168**

MISSISSIPPI BABY CASE, 2010

Two days after Cirila Baltazar-Cruz, a Mexican immigrant, gave birth in a Mississippi hospital in 2008, her newborn daughter was taken from her by state welfare workers on the basis of false allegations made by a hospital worker. The mother, who spoke an indigenous language and virtually no English or Spanish, could not defend herself against the charges. The SPLC succeeded in reuniting the mother and daughter after a year of separation, and filed suit against the state, the hospital and several employees. In a preliminary ruling, a federal judge wrote that the case was "riddled" with evidence of misconduct.

GEORGIA IMMIGRATION RAID, 2006
Testifying before a subcommittee of the U.S. House of Representatives in 2008, SPLC client Marie Justeen Mancha, 17, described her terror when federal immigration agents burst into her home in southeast Georgia two years earlier as she was preparing for school. An SPLC lawsuit alleged that Immigration and Customs Enforcement agents illegally detained, searched and harassed Latinos such as Mancha solely because of their appearance. "I started to hear the words, 'Police! Illegals!'" said Mancha, a U.S. citizen. "It seems as if those words still ring in my head today, giving me that fear of them busting into my home. I walked around the corner from the hallway and saw a tall man reach toward his gun and look straight at me."

TENNESSEE CHEESE WORKERS CASE, 2007

After repeatedly being underpaid and having their paychecks delayed for weeks, more than a dozen Mexican workers at Durrett Cheese Sales, a cheese-processing factory in Manchester, Tennessee, refused to leave the break room until they were paid. After they were fired and still refused to leave, the company called the sheriff, and they were thrown in jail. SPLC lawyers secured their release and sued the company and the sheriff in federal court for subjecting the workers to illegal retaliation and discrimination. The workers also had been subjected to a hostile work environment, where they were referred to as "stupid Indians" and "donkeys." SPLC clients Sarai Contreras Martinez is shown here, at home, with her disabled daughter. In a victory for workers, a federal court found that law enforcement officials can be found liable for retaliation if they knowingly act on behalf of an employer to suppress the federal rights of employees—a precedent that could be used in future cases. A settlement was reached on behalf of the workers.

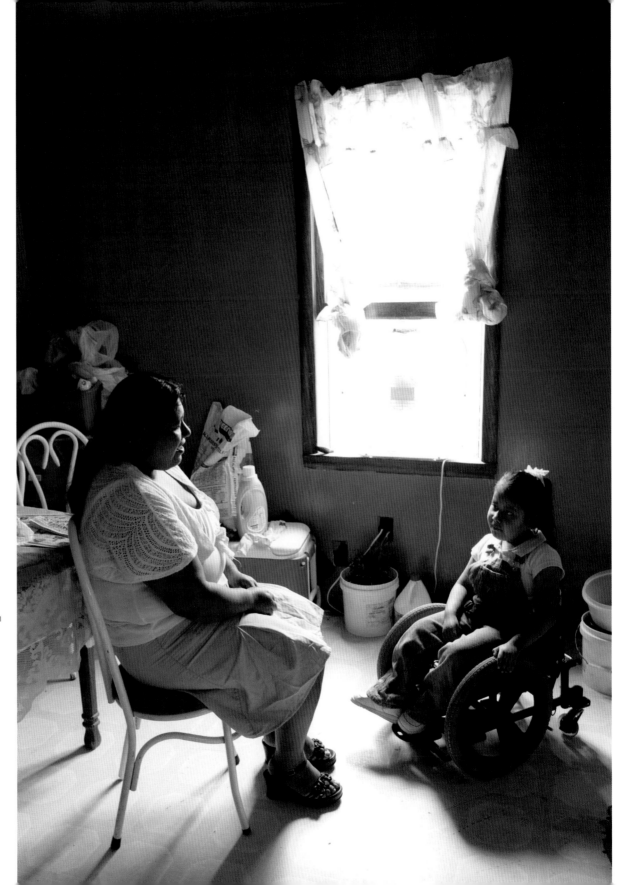

THE FILIPINO TEACHER CASE, 2010

Ingrid Cruz (left) and Mairi Nunag-Tañedo were among three hundred and sixty teachers from the Philippines lured to teach in Louisiana public schools under a federal guest worker program. Most borrowed money to pay about $16,000 in recruiting fees. When they arrived, they were forced to sign away an additional portion of their salaries under threat of being sent home and losing their original investment. Working with the American Federation of Teachers, the SPLC filed suit, alleging the teachers were ensnared in a "psychologically coercive and financially ruinous trafficking scheme that subjected teachers to exorbitant debt and forced labor." In 2012, a federal judge ordered labor recruiter Universal Placement International of Los Angeles and its owner to pay $4.5 million to the teachers.

HELPING A VICTIM OF WORKPLACE SEXUAL ASSAULT

Immigrant women are often unable to protect themselves from sexual harassment and assault in the workplace. In 2009, the SPLC filed suit against a yarn factory in North Carolina on behalf of Lilia Ixtlahuaca Martinez, who was brutally assaulted by the plant manager after she had earlier reported his harassment to company officials. During the attack, she was dragged across the floor by her hair as she tried to escape. She collapsed outside the building and was taken to a hospital by ambulance. The suit resulted in a $230,000 settlement and reforms to company policies.

given to a local white couple, both of whom practiced law before the very judge who approved the child's removal. Dees was outraged by what he considered the blatant theft of a newborn, and believed this was just one example of many transgressions against vulnerable immigrants occurring across the country.

The SPLC filed a federal lawsuit and succeeded in reuniting the desperate mother with her daughter after a full year of separation. The SPLC suit also sparked an investigation by the U.S. Department of Health and Human Services, which concluded "that this may be how business is conducted [in Mississippi] and that this is not an isolated incident."

As anti-immigrant fervor continued to build, state legislatures began passing harsh laws designed to drive immigrants from their states, or "self deport." These laws were crafted largely by lawyers who had worked for the very nativist groups the SPLC had earlier exposed as being tied to white supremacists. Arizona led the way in 2010 with Senate Bill 1070, a statute that made it a crime to be present in the state without proper documentation and required police to ask for immigration papers during routine traffic stops if they suspected someone of being undocumented. The law also imposed criminal penalties on anyone who hired, transported or harbored an unauthorized immigrant.

In the following year, five more states followed Arizona's example. Nowhere was the new legislation more draconian than in Alabama, where legislators forged it amid a legislative debate rife with stereotypes, incendiary rhetoric and bigotry aimed at a tiny sliver of the state's population. The chief Senate sponsor told colleagues they need to "empty the clip" to deal with immigrants. In the House, the sponsor used "Hispanic" and "illegal immigrant" interchangeably, an egregious error later cited by a federal judge.

In addition to Arizona's "papers please" provision, Alabama's legislature added cruel new elements. The law required school officials to determine whether enrolling children were born within the United States or were the children of undocumented immigrants. It criminalized common interactions with the undocumented. It made it a felony for the undocumented to enter into business transactions with the state. And it nullified private contracts with undocumented immigrants.

Alabama's law, known as H.B. 56, not only guaranteed racial profiling but encouraged the harassment and intimidation of all Latinos in the state. Concerned about the unconstitutional nature of the law, and the human rights violations that would follow, the SPLC filed suit in federal court. It also joined a coalition of civil rights groups suing the states of Georgia and South Carolina for enacting similar measures.

In the first week after Alabama's H.B. 56 went into effect, more than a thousand calls came in to a special hotline the SPLC established, reporting fear, discrimination, intimidation and other abuses. Within six months, five thousand calls from Latinos had been received. The law had unleashed a torrent of vigilantism, leading Alabamians to believe they could cheat, harass and intimidate Latinos with impunity.

Enrique Corral, a U.S. citizen, put it this way: "Hateful people are hateful no matter what, but with this law they feel more empowered. If I used to just spit on you, now I'm going to spit on you and kick you when you're down."

Thousands of children were kept home from school by frightened parents. Latino farmworkers fled the state, leaving crops rotting in the fields and farmers absorbing millions in losses.

Among those affected were a family with three small children whose water connection was shut off because they couldn't provide immigration documents; a day laborer whose employer flashed a gun rather than pay the wages she was owed; a family

CONTINUED ON **PAGE 172**

ALABAMA ANTI-IMMIGRANT LAW, 2011
Marchers in front of the Alabama Capitol protest H.B. 56, a harsh anti-immigrant law called "cruel, destructive and embarrassing"—the "worst in the nation"—by The New York Times. The SPLC launched a broad legal and education campaign to overturn the 2011 law, which promoted racial profiling, criminalized everyday interactions with undocumented immigrants, required schools to determine whether schoolchildren were born within the U.S. or had undocumented parents, and more. The SPLC's lawsuit succeeded in gutting most of the key elements of the law and significantly limited racial profiling under its "papers, please" provision.

THE VICTIMS OF ALABAMA'S WAR ON IMMIGRANTS

Alabama's anti-immigrant law in 2011 unleashed a torrent of vigilantism, leading Alabamians to believe they could cheat, harass and intimidate Latinos with impunity. The SPLC set up a special hotline so that Latinos could report the abuses they faced—resulting in more than a thousand calls in the first week. Nineteen-year-old Martha (left, with her son Julio) was jailed after being stopped for a minor traffic violation. Another family (sons pictured, middle) had a recently purchased car repossessed even though the payments were up to date— because the law invalidated contracts with an undocumented person. Carmen Velez (right) had difficulty renewing her car tag, even though she is a U.S. citizen, because a clerk would not accept her Puerto Rican birth certificate.

whose car was repossessed even though the payments were up to date; a teen who needed emergency surgery after being refused treatment at a hospital.

As these nightmares unfolded, the SPLC sought relief in federal court—and won. The courts blocked most of the Alabama law's provisions, including the chilling requirement for schoolchildren to verify their parents' immigration status. Key provisions of South Carolina's and Georgia's laws were blocked as well.

In October 2013, the SPLC announced a final settlement that gutted Alabama's law. Earlier, *The New York Times* had called it "cruel, destructive and embarrassing"—"the worst in the nation." Now, the headline on its editorial about the SPLC victory read, simply: "Alabama Surrenders."

Following the victory, Dees thanked the SPLC supporters who had made it all possible. "The law undermined our most fundamental ideals as a nation," he said. "This victory will have a major impact on many lives—not just immigrants, but legal residents and U.S. citizens who could be suspected of being unauthorized simply because they are Latino." He pledged to continue to work for comprehensive reform in Congress so that "no other state will be tempted to pass such a mean-spirited law again."

By 2014, though the ideologically divided Congress continued to push comprehensive reform down the road, no other state had passed a law like Alabama's.

ON SEPTEMBER 4, 2013, Attorney General Eric Holder wrote to House Speaker John Boehner to tell him the Obama administration would no longer enforce a provision of federal law that effectively denied certain spousal benefits to U.S. veterans in same-sex marriages.

The decision to stop enforcing a federal law, Holder noted, was "appropriately rare."

But days earlier, a federal court in California had ruled in an SPLC case that provisions of Title 38 governing the eligibility of veterans and their families to receive benefits were unconstitutional. The court said there was no legitimate reason to single out veterans for discrimination because of their sexual orientation. Weeks earlier, the U.S. Supreme Court had struck down the similarly discriminatory Defense of Marriage Act but had said nothing about the Title 38 provisions at issue in the SPLC case.

It had been forty years since the SPLC's landmark victory in the Frontiero case forced the U.S. military to provide the same benefits to servicewomen as did to men. Now, another barrier to equality had been shattered.

The decision meant that LGBT veterans would no longer be treated as second-class citizens by the Department of Veterans Affairs. And it brought a measure of security to the SPLC's client, Tracey Cooper-Harris.

Tracey had served twelve years in the Army, some of it in the Middle East supporting the wars in Afghanistan and Iraq, before her honorable discharge in 2003. After her service ended, she married her partner, Maggie, in California, where same-sex marriages were legal. Then she was diagnosed with multiple sclerosis, a debilitating neurological disease that the VA determined was related to her military service. She received disability benefits, but the VA refused to approve the additional compensation to which married veterans were entitled—benefits intended to ensure financial stability for spouses. The denial also meant the couple could not be buried together in a national veterans cemetery.

The SPLC victory changed all of that. But it was just one of the ways the organization fought for the rights of the LGBT community.

Violence against the LGBT community was a particular concern of the SPLC, in keeping with its work

CONTINUED ON **PAGE 177**

VETERANS BENEFITS DISCRIMINATION CASE, 2012
Tracey Cooper-Harris (left) served for twelve years in the U.S. Army and, afterward, married her partner, Maggie, in California, where same-sex marriages were legal. Then Tracey was diagnosed with multiple sclerosis related to her service. But the Department of Veterans Affairs denied her the full range of benefits for married, disabled veterans because federal law prevented the government from recognizing the couple's marriage. The SPLC sued on her behalf, and a federal judge found the VA's rules discriminatory and unconstitutional. Shortly thereafter, the Obama administration announced it would no longer enforce the provision of federal law upon which the VA rule was based.

TWO SPLC CLIENTS, BOTH TRAILBLAZERS, MEET IN 2012
When the SPLC filed suit to help Tracey Cooper-Harris (left)
gain veterans benefits for same-sex couples, she and Joe Levin
appeared at a Washington, D.C., press conference with former
SPLC client Sharron Cohen (formerly Frontiero) to highlight
the similarities between the cases. As a young Air Force officer in 1970, Frontiero was denied certain housing benefits that
were routinely granted to men. Her case, handled by Levin,
went to the U.S. Supreme Court and was the first successful
sex discrimination case against the federal government.

SEX DISCRIMINATION IN VETERANS PROGRAM, 2012

Emily Bagby was a veteran of the U.S. Army who found herself homeless during a period of unemployment. For help, she turned to the Asheville Buncombe Community Christian Ministry in North Carolina, which received federal money to provide job training programs and other classes for veterans. But the ministry didn't allow women to attend the work-training classes for men, such as truck driving or culinary arts. Instead, women were offered training in such things as knitting, art therapy, yoga, meditation, self-esteem and Bible study.

LGBT SCHOOL BULLYING CASE, 2011

In the Anoka-Hennepin school district, Minnesota's largest, teachers were prohibited from even discussing issues related to LGBT people. In practice, this meant that teachers and administrators failed to stand up for children who were being routinely harassed—and sometimes physically assaulted—because of their sexual orientation. At the time, news outlets across the country were filled with stories of gay and lesbian children taking their own lives because of the abuses they faced at school. Anoka-Hennepin schools had lost four students to suicide in an eight-month period. The SPLC sued the district on behalf of four students, including 14-year-old Kyle Rooker, who didn't identify as gay but endured abuse because he didn't sufficiently conform to traditional gender roles. In 2012, district officials signed a consent decree to settle the suit, agreeing to a wide-ranging plan to protect LGBT students from harassment. The plaintiffs were honored for their courage by Attorney General Eric Holder.

spanning decades to hold white supremacist groups accountable for violence against minorities. In the late 1990s, several shocking crimes brought national attention to anti-gay hate crime. In 1998, 21-year-old Matthew Shepard was tortured, tied to a fence and left to die in a remote area near Laramie, Wyoming. And the next year, in the SPLC's own backyard, 39-year-old Billy Jack Gaither of Sylacauga, Alabama, was brutally beaten to death—his throat slashed and body bludgeoned with an axe handle—before being tossed on a pile of burning tires.

The SPLC honored Gaither's memory in its Civil Rights Memorial Center, along with the martyrs of the civil rights movement. But that was only a beginning.

In the years that followed, the SPLC launched a vigorous campaign, both in the courts and in the classrooms, to stem an epidemic of anti-LGBT bullying and harassment in the nation's schools. Across the country, the headlines screamed with stories of gay and lesbian children dying from suicide after being bullied.

Ground zero in the campaign was the Anoka-Hennepin school district just northwest of Minneapolis, where at least four students took their own lives between November 2009 and July 2010. Anti-LGBT bullying was suspected in each case.

One of the students was Samantha Johnson, just 13 and in the seventh grade. In the months preceding her suicide, Samantha had been depressed. Previously a good student, she had begun to fail classes and had dropped out of volleyball. One day, she laid down in the bathtub at her home, put the barrel of a shotgun in her mouth and pulled the trigger.

Brittany Geldert, her best friend, knew firsthand the kind of relentless abuse that Samantha had endured. Both were tomboys, openly bisexual, and bullied at school because of it. Brittany was repeatedly tripped and pushed into lockers and trash cans.

CONTINUED ON **PAGE 180**

LGBT RIGHTS FOR STUDENTS, 2011
Desiree Shelton (left) and Aiden Lindstrom were selected by their classmates as "royalty" for the Snow Days winter events at Champlin Park High School in Minnesota. But the school altered the traditional festivities so that the pair could not walk together as a couple. The SPLC filed suit on their behalf to uphold their rights to freedom of expression under the First Amendment. Less than twenty-four hours later, school officials reversed their position.

TEACHING TOLERANCE FIGHTS SCHOOL BULLYING
In response to an epidemic of anti-LGBT bullying in schools across the country and a rash of student suicides, the SPLC's Teaching Tolerance project produced a classroom documentary recounting the powerful story of Jamie Nabozny, whose lawsuit led to a landmark court decision that held school officials accountable for not protecting students from abuse.

She was called names—"dyke," "whore," "skank," "slut" and worse. She was told she "should kill herself." Even though she reported the harassment more than thirty times to school administrators, little was done to protect her. Eventually, she became depressed and thought about suicide, too. Her grades suffered, and she left school for a month to try to recover. "It was like I was trapped in a nightmare and could never wake up," she said.

Another district student, Kyle Rooker, didn't identify as gay but faced similar bullying in middle school because he didn't conform to traditional gender roles and often wore feminine clothing. Verbal insults evolved into physical assaults. He was slapped, shoved into walls and lockers and, once, urinated on in the restroom. "When I would walk down the hall, I would cover my face because I was so afraid," he said. But just as Brittany found out, his desperate appeals to school officials did nothing to stop the harassment. He and other LGBT students were told to avoid the bullies, to just "lay low" or "try to stay out of people's way."

The intolerance in the Anoka-Hennepin school district was no accident. The 38,000-student district, Minnesota's largest, was in the heart of U.S. Rep. Michele Bachmann's congressional district. Bachmann, an anti-LGBT crusader, had helped make schools a battleground over what she and her allies called a "homosexual agenda" and had vigorously opposed efforts to make campuses more tolerant. Responding to community concerns, the district had adopted a policy requiring teachers and other personnel to remain "neutral" about issues involving homosexuality, essentially preventing teachers from addressing the bigotry and hostility.

As the crisis in Anoka-Hennepin grew, the SPLC agreed to represent several students in the school district and began to investigate the harassment. At the same time, in the fall of 2010, the SPLC debuted its new Teaching Tolerance classroom documentary, *Bullied: A Student, a School and a Case that Made History*. It told the powerful story of Jamie Nabozny. His lawsuit led to a landmark 1996 federal court decision that held school officials accountable for failing to protect him. The film was designed not only to show students the terrible toll bullying could take on its victims but also to remind teachers and administrators of their responsibility to create safer school environments for all students. (Within two years, the SPLC had distributed more than one hundred thousand free copies to schools across the country and was flooded with comments about its impact on students.)

Nowhere was the film more relevant than in the Anoka-Hennepin district. In an attempt to gain public support for reform, the SPLC in November 2010 hosted a special screening in Minneapolis, one attended by more than two thousand people.

But district officials were unmoved. So six months later, SPLC lawyers upped the ante, demanding that the district repeal its "neutrality" policy or face a federal lawsuit that would force its hand.

"The mandatory silence imposed by the policy leaves teachers without tools to handle LGBT bullying and creates an atmosphere in which LGBT students are isolated and feel unprotected," the SPLC lawyers wrote. Further, the policy violated the Fourteenth Amendment's guarantee of equal protection under the law. "This fundamental constitutional guarantee prohibits school district officials from singling out any group of students for disfavored treatment based solely on their membership in an unpopular minority."

District officials again refused to take action, so in July the SPLC went to federal court on behalf of Geldert, Rooker and three other students. "For many years, these policies have deemed LGBT people, and them alone, as unworthy of being mentioned,

MISSISSIPPI ANTI-LGBT BULLYING CASE, 2013

Destin Holmes didn't feel welcome in her new school along Mississippi's Gulf Coast. No wonder: From the moment the eighth-grader arrived, she was taunted and mocked. Other children bombarded her with anti-gay slurs and insults, leading her to attempt suicide. Teachers even joined in, singling her out because of her sexual orientation. One wouldn't let her use the girl's bathroom; another wouldn't let her participate in an exercise where the class was divided by gender. The principal called her a "pathetic fool" and said he didn't "want a dyke in this school." An SPLC suit was pending in 2014.

IN MEMORY OF ALL THE CHILDREN
WHOSE LIVES WERE LOST BECAUSE
OF BULLYING.

SPLC FILM DRAWS THOUSANDS, 2010

Tammy Aaberg spoke at a viewing of the SPLC classroom documentary *Bullied: A Student, a School and a Case that Made History* in Minneapolis, attended by more than two thousand people. The film was designed to show the terrible toll bullying could take and remind teachers of their responsibility to create safe classroom environments. It was dedicated to 11-year-old Carl Walker (top right), who hung himself in 2009 after being bullied by other children in Springfield, Massachusetts. The SPLC later pursued legal action against Minnesota's Anoka-Hennepin School District, where 15-year-old Justin Aaberg (bottom right) took his own life in 2010. More than one hundred thousand free copies of *Bullied* were distributed within two years, and a flood of comments from educators and students affirmed its positive impact.

let alone protected, in District classrooms," the suit alleged. In addition, the suit charged, it was clear that the policy existed only because of "community animus" toward LGBT people.

The case would never reach trial. In March 2012, the school district reached a settlement with the SPLC, agreeing to repeal its policy and to implement a wide-ranging plan to protect LGBT children.

It was a milestone in the SPLC's battle to make schools safer for all children—one that reverberated across the country.

Brittany Geldert's parents thanked the SPLC for "giving us a voice that has circled the globe. ... This experience has shown us that there is always someone willing to help, that we are not alone when we are fighting for what's right. It gives us great pride and hope in mankind."

Tammy Aaberg, who lost her 15-year-old son, Justin, to suicide in the district in 2010, wrote, "Your work in Anoka-Hennepin has provided hope for so many. My sincere wish is that students who feel hopeless in the face of bullying—who feel they have no one left to turn to—will see what the Southern Poverty Law Center did in Anoka-Hennepin and know there are adults who care about them—adults willing to fight for them."

In the months that followed, SPLC lawyers challenged numerous schools in the Deep South that were violating the constitutional rights of students by insisting that they conform to traditional gender norms. At the same time, the SPLC trained its sights on another serious problem that was harming LGBT youth—a practice called "conversion therapy," also known as "reparative" or "ex-gay therapy," that was based on the notion that LGBT people could be cured of their sexual orientation.

In November 2012, the SPLC filed an innovative lawsuit accusing a New Jersey group, Jews Offering New Alternatives for Healing (JONAH), of violating that state's consumer fraud law. It was the first time a conversion therapy practitioner in the United States had been sued for fraudulent business practices.

The four young gay men represented by the SPLC described therapy sessions in which they were ridiculed as "faggots" and "homos" in mock locker room and gym class scenarios. They also were instructed to beat an effigy of their mother with a tennis racket, undress in front of other naked young men and older counselors, cuddle with other men, and go to bath houses in order to be nude with "father figures." When the plaintiffs did not experience a change in sexual orientation, therapists blamed them for not working hard enough. For this, the defendants and their parents paid as much as $10,000 a year.

Teens and young people across the country were being forced into conversion therapy, often against their will. The "therapy" not only failed to cure those subjected to it, it often left them with deep psychological scars.

Pushed mainly by the religious right, conversion therapy had been discredited or criticized by virtually all major American medical, psychiatric, psychological and professional counseling organizations. Beyond being ineffective, it encouraged a climate of bigotry by promoting the idea that homosexuality was a mental disorder or a personal choice.

The legal fight against conversion therapy was just beginning, and a resolution of the lawsuit against JONAH was, perhaps, years away. But the SPLC's work to champion the rights of the LGBT community was making a clear difference. It had put the SPLC at the forefront of one of the fiercest civil rights battles of the new century and was one more example of the organization fighting to uphold the rights of the most vulnerable members of society. •

FIGHTING FOR MARRIAGE EQUALITY, 2014

Paul Hard lost his husband in a car crash just three months after the couple was legally married in Massachusetts in 2011. But the state of Alabama, where he and David Fancher lived, refused to recognize the marriage. That subjected Hard to an array of indignities and meant he could not collect any proceeds from a pending wrongful death suit. In 2014, the SPLC filed a federal suit on his behalf to overturn the state's 1998 Marriage Protection Act and its Sanctity of Marriage Amendment, laws that also prevented the Alabama National Guard from providing benefits to same-sex spouses, despite a federal directive to do so.

SUIT OVERTURNS RACIST CHILD WELFARE POLICY, 1974

Margaret Ann Wambles sought the SPLC's help after child welfare workers in Montgomery, Alabama, took her 3-year-old child from her—without a hearing or due process—simply because she was unmarried and living with a black man. She had no criminal record and had never abused or neglected her child in any way. After the SPLC filed suit, a federal court struck down major portions of Alabama's child welfare law as unconstitutional, ruling that "family integrity" may not be disturbed absent evidence of real physical or emotional harm.

ALABAMA PROM CASE, 1994
Racial tensions flared at a high school in Wedowee, Alabama, after the principal threatened to cancel the prom if interracial couples planned to attend and told student Revonda Bowen that her parents' marriage was a "mistake." Later that year, someone set fire to the school, burning it to the ground. The SPLC won a settlement for Bowen, seen here with Morris Dees and her parents, Dorothy and Wayne Bowen. The SPLC suit shined a light on the racism and bigotry that persisted in many Deep South schools even thirty years after the Civil Rights Act outlawed Jim Crow segregation.

TEN COMMANDMENTS CASE, 2001

In the dead of night, Alabama Chief Justice Roy Moore secretly installed a 2.5-ton monument to the Ten Commandments in the rotunda of the state judicial building, violating the constitutional principle of separation of church and state. The SPLC sued Moore on behalf of a lawyer concerned his clients would not receive equal treatment if they did not share Moore's religious beliefs. The legal proceedings drew numerous demonstrators, including those who displayed the Confederate flag. A federal judge ordered the monument removed, but Moore refused. Moore was suspended, and the monument was moved out of the building. The Alabama Judicial Inquiry Commission later removed the judge from office for defying the court order.

EXPOSING PREDATORY LENDERS

In 2013, the SPLC launched a campaign to expose the practices of predatory lenders who trap low-income people in a cycle of high-interest, unaffordable debt. Among the victims was 68-year-old Ruby Frazier of Dothan, Alabama, who used her pickup truck to secure a title loan—at 300 percent interest—so she could help her struggling daughter pay bills. When her daughter didn't make timely payments, the debt quickly ballooned from $2,200 to $3,000 and a sheriff's deputy came to repossess her vehicle. "I go by what God said: 'Thou shalt not steal,'" she said. "And that's stealing."

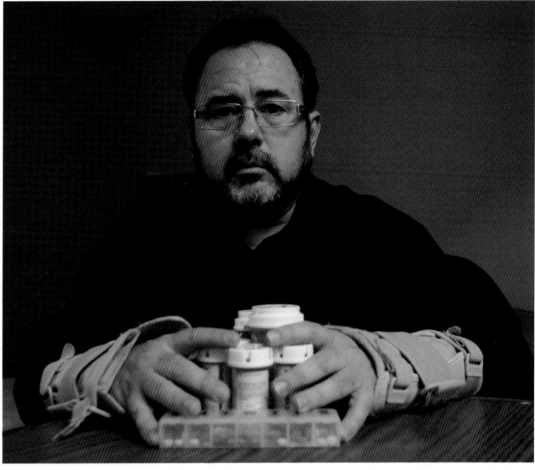

LANGUAGE DISCRIMINATION CASE, 1996

A tax collector in Madison County, Alabama, refused to sign a homestead exemption for Julio and Carmen Telleria, naturalized citizens from the Dominican Republic, because they did not speak English. He said they had to recite an oath in English, a requirement that applied only to foreign-born applicants. The SPLC filed suit and reached a settlement requiring the tax collector to stop his discriminatory policy and make other changes in the way he treated immigrants and minorities.

EXPOSING UNSAFE CONDITIONS IN POULTRY PLANTS

Oscar was fired from his poultry job in Alabama after he developed carpal tunnel syndrome and tendinitis, common injuries among poultry workers who face relentless pressure as they slice or cut chickens that zoom by on high-speed processing lines. In 2013, the SPLC exposed the grueling conditions for workers, many of them immigrants, and helped block a regulation that would have increased line speeds to 175 birds per minute.

...UNTIL JUSTICE ROLLS DOWN LIKE WATERS
AND RIGHTEOUSNESS LIKE A MIGHTY STREAM

MARTIN LUTHER KING JR

CHAPTER FOUR

'UNTIL JUSTICE ROLLS DOWN LIKE WATERS...'

Most of those who made the movement weren't the famous: they were the faceless. They weren't the noted; they were the nameless—the marchers with tired feet, the protesters beaten back by billy clubs and fire hoses, the unknown women and men who risked job and home and life.

—JULIAN BOND, NOVEMBER 5, 1989

BEFORE HER ACT OF DEFIANCE on a Montgomery, Alabama, bus in 1955, Rosa Parks was one of the many dedicated activists who rallied to the cause of ending American apartheid but were unknown to the world. Thirty-four years later, when she spoke outside the headquarters of the Southern Poverty Law Center, she was an icon whose arrest for refusing to give up her seat to a white passenger sparked the Montgomery bus boycott and lit an inextinguishable flame that ultimately consumed Jim Crow.

Six thousand people stood under a beaming sun on November 5, 1989, as Parks helped dedicate the Civil Rights Memorial, a monument to those who gave what Abraham Lincoln called the "last full measure of devotion" when he honored the dead on the blood-soaked battlefield of Gettysburg 126 years earlier.

Before her, on the round, black granite table of the Memorial, were inscribed the names of forty people who were murdered. Some, such as Dr. Martin Luther King Jr. and NAACP field secretary Medgar Evers, were assassinated because of their leadership roles. Others, like the Birmingham girls Addie Mae Collins, Denise McNair, Carole Robertson and Cynthia Wesley, were victims of terrorism committed by white supremacists intent on instilling fear in civil rights activists and the black community. Still others, like Emmett Till, were those whose deaths stirred the souls of millions by demonstrating the brutality and injustice faced by African Americans in the Deep South. Together, their deaths propelled a great movement.

In her address, Parks reminded the audience of the continuing struggle for justice.

"It never ends," she said. "But we are living in hope that the future, as we gather for peace, justice, good will and the priceless life of all, that we will not have to mourn the dead but rejoice in the fact that we, as a nation of peace-loving people, will overcome any obstacle against us."

The Memorial was the brainchild of Morris Dees. In 1987, he was speaking at the annual convention of the Alabama NAACP, where he was being honored for the SPLC's court victory over the United Klans of America just weeks earlier. An all-white jury in Mobile, Alabama, had awarded $7 million to the SPLC's client, Beulah Mae Donald, the mother of a black teen who was kidnapped and murdered by Klansmen.

CIVIL RIGHTS MEMORIAL DEDICATION
Julian Bond examines the names of forty civil rights martyrs with renowned activist Rosa Parks on November 5, 1989—the day the SPLC dedicated the Civil Rights Memorial in Montgomery, Alabama. Bonds' speech to the crowd concluded with a call to action for future generations: "We must continue to fight. Next to those we honor today, we are called to give comparatively little—our time, our energy, our caring."

**PLANNING AND BUILDING
THE CIVIL RIGHTS MEMORIAL**
The SPLC persuaded Maya Lin (right, with SPLC President Richard Cohen) to design a memorial to honor those slain during the civil rights movement. The daughter of Chinese immigrants, Lin had earlier gained fame for designing the Vietnam Veterans Memorial in Washington, D.C., while a student at Yale. World-famous stone cutter John Benson (above right) used his own lettering design to inscribe Dr. King's inspiring words on the Memorial.

At the meeting, Dees recited part of the closing argument he had delivered, in which he said that when the "final roll is called in heaven," the slain Michael Donald would take his place alongside Dr. King and other fallen martyrs of the movement. After the speech, he was approached by several young people in the audience who weren't familiar with some of the names he had mentioned, names like Medgar Evers, Viola Liuzzo and Emmett Till. During the drive back to Montgomery that night, Dees was troubled that they knew so little about such an important—and recent—part of the nation's history. Racism, sometimes veiled but plain as day to those who recalled the earlier bloodshed, was creeping back more and more into the mainstream political discourse as another presidential election loomed. After he received the GOP nomination for president in 1980, for example, Ronald Reagan gave his first speech in Philadelphia, Mississippi, where the Klan had murdered three civil rights workers sixteen years earlier. He spoke of restoring "states' rights," a phrase fraught with echoes of the pre-civil rights South and seen by many as a continuation of Richard Nixon's "Southern strategy" of appealing to the resentment felt by some whites to the gains of African Americans.

The nation, Dees thought, needed a permanent reminder of the sacrifices paid by so many to end nearly a century of Jim Crow segregation.

The Memorial would stand right in front of the SPLC building that had been completed in 1985 after Klansmen firebombed the organization's office two years earlier. To design it, SPLC officials called upon the artist and architectural designer Maya Lin. The daughter of Chinese immigrants, Lin had gained fame in 1982 for designing the Vietnam Veterans Memorial in Washington, D.C., while still a student at Yale University. Since then, she had not worked on any other memorials. She was hesitant to respond to the SPLC's overture, she wrote in her book *Boundaries*, because she didn't want to be "typecast" as a monument designer. But when she found out there were no other memorials to the dead of the civil rights movement, she put her qualms aside.

Lin spent months researching the movement and was shocked that so much violence had occurred. "[B]ut I was even more disturbed that the information I was learning about our history—events that were going on while I was growing up—was never taught to me in school."

MAYA LIN, CIVIL RIGHTS MEMORIAL DESIGNER
Maya Lin stands on the upper level of the Civil Rights Memorial during the dedication ceremony in 1989. She envisioned the plaza as "a contemplative area—a place to remember the civil rights movement, to honor those killed during the struggle, to appreciate how far the country has come in its quest for equality, and to consider how far it has to go." The circular black granite table below records the names of the martyrs and chronicles the history of the movement in lines that radiate like the hands of a clock. The sight and sound of the rippling water compel visitors to trace the martyrs' names as they see reflections of their own faces.

While en route to Montgomery to visit the site for the first time, she came across a quotation from Dr. King's "I have a dream" speech in which he paraphrased Amos 5:24: "We are not satisfied and we will not be satisfied until justice rolls down like waters and righteousness like a mighty stream." Lin had found the inspiration she needed. "Immediately I knew that the memorial would be about water and that these words would connect the past with the future," Lin wrote. "By the time I arrived at the site, I had an idea of what I wanted to do. I remember my first luncheon with Morris Dees and members of the center, and the proverbial sketch on a napkin, which I had quickly drawn on the airplane ride down, came out." After the meeting, she returned to New York to begin working on drawings and models.

A few months later, a design and description of the project were presented to the media. The Memorial would consist of an upper and lower plaza. On the upper part, a thin sheet of water would flow from a quiet pool down the face of a curved, black granite wall. It would be nine feet high and forty feet long and inscribed with the quotation from Dr. King's most famous speech. The lower plaza would contain a twelve-foot-wide circular granite table, with water emerging from the center and flowing evenly across the surface. On the surface of the table, beneath the flowing water, a circular timeline, reminiscent of a sundial, would tell the story of major events of the civil rights movement and of those who died.

"In choosing to intertwine events with people's deaths, I was trying to illustrate the cause-and-effect relationship between them," Lin wrote. "The struggle for civil rights in this country was a people's movement, and a walk around the table reveals how often the act of a single person—often enough, a single death—was followed by a new and better law. So many of the victims we don't know about, so many of the people we never heard about. What this movement was really about was the acts of an entire people. The Montgomery bus boycott is just one of many examples of this."

While Lin planned the Memorial, SPLC researchers began combing through newspaper clippings and death certificates from the era, the archives of civil rights groups, FBI documents and other records in an attempt to identify the names that should be engraved on the Memorial. With the understanding that the roots of the struggle reached back for decades, the SPLC chose to focus on those who were murdered during the most pivotal and contentious era of the civil rights movement, the period between the U.S. Supreme Court's school desegregation decision in *Brown v. Board of Education* on May 17, 1954, and the assassination of Dr. King on April 4, 1968.

In the end, the research yielded forty names, though there were countless suspicious deaths. Those selected ranged in age from 11 to 66. They were students, farmers, ministers, truck drivers, a homemaker, a deputy sheriff and a Nobel laureate. Thirty-two were black. Eight were white. "Each name is a history lesson, and we are saying, don't just think of the deaths, but think of a movement of ordinary people who just got tired of injustice," Dees told *The New York Times* in 1989.

Some of the names—like James Chaney, Andrew Goodman and Michael Schwerner, the civil rights workers murdered by Klansmen in Philadelphia, Mississippi, in 1964—were well known. Others were not. Few around the country, for example, had heard of the remarkable bravery of Reverend George Lee, a Baptist minister in the Mississippi Delta town of Belzoni who began preaching about voting in the early 1950s. Lee formed a local chapter of the NAACP and worked to register African-American voters in a county where there were none. He was warned to stop, but refused. On May 7, 1955, while driving home,

he was shot in the face and died. Local authorities ruled that Lee was fatally injured in a traffic accident and that the lead pellets found in his face and neck were probably from dental fillings that had come loose. No one was ever charged for killing him.

The location for the Memorial, in the middle of the Cradle of the Confederacy—a place that was infamous during the movement for midnight bombings, the beating of Freedom Riders and other horrors—could not have been more appropriate. As Julian Bond noted in his keynote address at the dedication, it stood just a few blocks west of the first Capitol of the Confederacy, the spot where Jefferson Davis was inaugurated and later gave the order to attack Fort Sumter, and just a few blocks east of Court Square in downtown Montgomery, where Rosa Parks had boarded the bus for her historic ride and where slaves had once been auctioned. And from where Bond spoke, it seemed as if he could almost touch the steeple of the Dexter Avenue King Memorial Baptist Church, where Dr. King had led the bus boycott, just a few hundred feet away.

"Once, this cradle rocked with the violence of our opponents; today it is soothed by the waters of this monument," Bond said. "A monument which, like the movement it honors, is majestic in its simplicity, overwhelming in its power. It bears the names of forty men, women, and children who gave their lives for freedom. It recalls their individual sacrifice. And it summons us to continue their collective cause."

That recollection ... that summoning ... was exactly what Dees had in mind.

CIVIL RIGHTS ACTIVISTS filled the crowd at the dedication, as did relatives of the men, women and children whose names were engraved on the Memorial. Among the family members who addressed the crowd was Mamie Till Mobley. Her

FORTY MARTYRS
On the Civil Rights Memorial are inscribed the names of individuals who lost their lives in the struggle for freedom during the modern civil rights movement—1954 to 1968. These were the years from the U.S. Supreme Court ruling in *Brown v. Board of Education* to Dr. King's assassination. The forty martyrs include activists who were targeted for death because of their civil rights work; random victims of white supremacists determined to halt the movement; and individuals who, in the sacrifice of their own lives, brought new awareness to the brutality and injustice faced by African Americans in the South. Pictures are not available for two of the martyrs.
SEE PAGE 228 FOR THEIR NAMES AND STORIES.

LEST WE FORGET
Kimberly Robinson touches her grandfather's name—Herbert Lee—on the Memorial during the dedication ceremony. On a day of tears and memories in a city forever linked to both the Civil War and the civil rights movement, hundreds of family members filled the streets around the nation's only memorial to those lynched, beaten, bombed or shot because they were African-American or because they were white and helping in the fight for equality.

son Emmett was just 14 when he left Chicago to visit cousins in Mississippi in 1955.

He was abducted after he supposedly whistled or said something disrespectful to a white woman, and his horribly disfigured body was found three days later floating in the Tallahatchie River. As was customary in such cases, the two men charged with his murder—one of whom later admitted his guilt to a magazine writer—were acquitted by an all-white jury.

Ms. Mobley was overcome with emotion when she touched the Memorial. "I ran my fingers over the letters of Emmett's name and felt the cool water," she later wrote in *Death of Innocence: The Story of the Hate Crime That Changed America*. "I began to weep. ... It was like touching my son. Like reliving his funeral. But, as I told people there, it also filled me with such joy to see Emmett being honored, to see him included among the martyrs of the movement."

Denise McNair, whose name also was etched into the Memorial, would have been nearing her thirty-eighth birthday that day. But she and three other little girls were cut down in 1963 by a bomb planted by Klansmen at Birmingham's 16th Street Baptist Church. Chris McNair told the crowd at the dedication that his daughter had wanted to join the fight for freedom that was roiling their city. "I remember she was in the seventh grade, and everybody was marching in Birmingham and going to jail, and Denise wanted to march, and she said to her mother, 'I want to march.'" But she was too little, they told her.

Also there was Dr. Caroline Goodman, whose son Andrew, an anthropology student from New York, answered the call by volunteering for the "Freedom Summer" voting rights project in Mississippi in 1964. His murder, along with those of fellow civil rights activists James Chaney and Michael Schwerner, inspired the 1988 film *Mississippi Burning*. Dr. Goodman recalled the day her son's body was found buried in an earthen dam near the

MAMIE TILL MOBLEY AT DEDICATION
On the day of the Civil Rights Memorial's dedication, the mother of civil rights martyr Emmett Till tearfully said it was like reaching out and touching her son again. "It's almost as if I'm reliving the funeral," Mamie Till Mobley said, "and yet my heart is full of joy that not only my son but all of these other people who gave their lives for such a great cause are getting the recognition that is their due."

spot where the three young men were shot execution-style by Klansmen. "When Andy's body was found, his father, now dead, said, 'Our grief, though personal, belongs to our nation. This tragedy is not private. It is part of the public consciousness of our country.' And this extraordinary monument has etched these losses in stone, and will be a lasting reminder of the courage and commitment to generations yet unborn."

There was Ellie Dahmer, the widow of Vernon Dahmer, a wealthy black businessman who lived near Hattiesburg, Mississippi. On the night of January 10, 1966, after announcing on the radio the day before that he was raising money to pay the poll taxes for African Americans who wanted to vote but could not afford it, he awoke to the sound of explosions and gunfire. "As we slept," Ms. Dahmer recalled, "our house was firebombed by the Klansmen. Our only escape was through the windows because the doors of our house were burning. Vernon died that same afternoon ... because of the fumes he inhaled while he stayed in the house to return the Klansmen's fire."

And there was Samuel Younge Sr., the father of Samuel Younge Jr., a student and civil rights organizer at Alabama's prestigious Tuskegee Institute who was shot in the head by a service station attendant after he argued about being directed to the "colored" restroom. Younge noted that his son's strong "desire for equality" was evident early in life. He resented using separate water fountains, toilets and lunch counters. "On motor trips, he said we would not buy gas unless he could use the white restroom." Once he was in college, he devoted himself full time to the movement—helping to organize pickets and sit-ins, fighting for equal city services, coming to the aid of tenant farmers who were run off their land because of their civil rights activities, and much more. "To Sammy, his biggest joy ... was getting hundreds of blacks registered to vote. It was his voter registration work and his desire to integrate public facilities that led to his death."

Sixteen years after the dedication, in 2005, the SPLC added a major educational component to the Memorial by opening the Civil Rights Memorial Center. It immediately became a powerful teaching tool. Each year, thousands of schoolchildren from around the country visit the Memorial and the Civil Rights Memorial Center, where they learn about the civil rights martyrs and the events of the movement through interactive exhibits and a twenty-minute film, *Faces in the Water*. On their way out, visitors can publicly pledge to work for justice, equality and human rights in their own lives by adding their names to the Wall of Tolerance, a digital cascade of multicolored names falling, like the water on the Memorial outside, down the face of a massive, curved black wall.

Within a year of its opening, twenty-four thousand people had visited the Civil Rights Memorial Center, and the numbers grew each year. Within the first eight years, more than six hundred thousand people, many of them supporters of the SPLC, had placed their names on the Wall of Tolerance. Among them was Congressman John Lewis, the Alabama native who had been clubbed by state troopers while leading a voting rights march across the Edmund Pettus Bridge in Selma on March 7, 1965—a day that became known as Bloody Sunday and that led, after the march's ultimate completion in Montgomery more than three weeks later, to passage of the Voting Rights Act. Each year, sponsored by the Faith & Politics Institute, Lewis leads members of Congress on a tour of civil rights landmarks. On some of those tours, they visit the Civil Rights Memorial on the anniversary of Bloody Sunday and lay a wreath on the names etched there in granite.

CONTINUED ON **PAGE 206**

THOUSANDS ATTEND DEDICATION CEREMONY

Six thousand people—including more than six hundred family members of the civil rights martyrs—gathered in Montgomery on November 5, 1989, to witness the dedication of the new Civil Rights Memorial. The SPLC's first president, Julian Bond, gave the keynote address. Other speakers included Rosa Parks (seen with Morris Dees in 1995); Martin Luther King III; Mamie Till Mobley, mother of civil rights martyr Emmett Till; Chris McNair, father of civil rights martyr Denise McNair; and Myrlie Evers, widow of Medgar Evers.

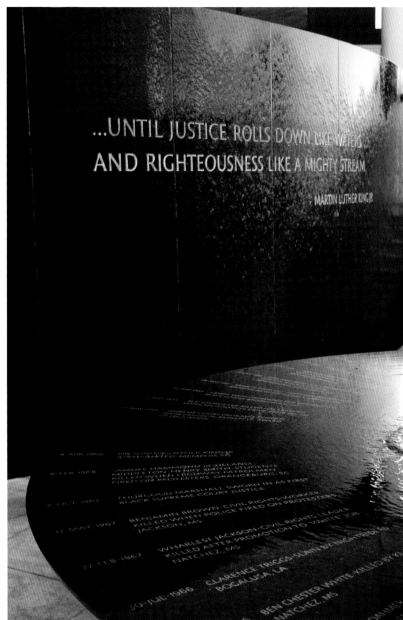

ON JUNE 12, 2007, SPLC President Richard Cohen sat alongside Myrlie Evers, the widow of Medgar Evers, before the U.S. House Subcommittee on Crime, Terrorism and Homeland Security. He was testifying in support of the Emmett Till Unsolved Civil Rights Crime Act, which would fund a special Department of Justice effort to re-examine the many unsolved murders of the civil rights era.

Cohen told the subcommittee that when the SPLC unveiled the Civil Rights Memorial few of the killers in the civil rights-era cases had been prosecuted or convicted. Some of the accused had been tried and acquitted by all-white juries even when the evidence of their guilt was overwhelming. The 1989 dedication, Cohen said, had been "tinged with sadness, not simply because those remembered on the Memorial had lost their lives, but because most of the family members in attendance still awaited justice for the killing of their loved one."

"The reason justice has not been served was the callous indifference, and often the criminal collusion, of many white law enforcement officials in the segregated South," Cohen said. "There simply was no justice for blacks during the civil rights era. The whole criminal justice system from the police, to the prosecutors, to the juries, and to the judges, was perverted by racial bigotry. Blacks were routinely beaten, bombed and shot with impunity. Sometimes, the killers picked their victims on a whim. Sometimes, they targeted them for their activism. In some cases, prominent white citizens were involved. Herbert Lee of Liberty, Mississippi, for example, was shot in the head by a state legislator in broad daylight in 1961 and nothing was done."

There had been a few successful prosecutions in the aftermath of the bloody era. Alabama Attorney General Bill Baxley, for example, had reopened the investigation into the Birmingham church bombing, leading to the conviction of Klansman Robert "Dynamite" Chambliss for first-degree murder in 1977.

But if not for the renewed interest sparked by the Civil Rights Memorial, several of the killers probably never would have been brought to justice. Inspired by the Memorial, investigative journalist Jerry Mitchell used the SPLC book *Free At Last: A History of the Civil Rights Movement and Those Who Died in the Struggle* as a "road map on my journey into reinvestigating these cases," he recalled when he spoke at the dedication of the Civil Rights Memorial Center in 2005.

Mitchell's investigations prompted prosecutions that put four Klansmen behind bars—Byron De La Beckwith for assassinating Medgar Evers; Sam Bowers for ordering the fatal firebombing of Vernon Dahmer's house; Bobby Cherry for the Birmingham church bombing; and Edgar Ray Killen for helping to orchestrate the executions of Chaney, Goodman and Schwerner in the Mississippi Burning case. Following Cohen's and Evers' testimony and the passage of the Emmett Till Unsolved Civil Rights Crime Act, other killers were brought to justice.

"The Memorial," Mitchell explained, began as "a reminder that the martyrs' killers walked free, even though everyone knew they were guilty." But "[a]fter it was dedicated in 1989, it transformed into an instrument of justice."

As for the victims listed on the Memorial, eight white supremacists were convicted for thirteen of the forty murders in the years following the 1989 dedication. Four others were convicted in another Mississippi killing.

BY THE EARLY 1990s, Dees and the SPLC team had racked up impressive victories against the Klan and other violent white supremacist groups. But Dees knew that a legal campaign, while effective, was not enough. More needed to be done to fight the bigotry that divided the country and led to violent hate

CONTINUED ON **PAGE 211**

PAYING HOMAGE
SPLC President Richard Cohen (far left) joins hands with Ethel Kennedy and others, including Congressman John Lewis and Kerry Kennedy, around the Civil Rights Memorial in 2012. Members of Congress and other dignitaries frequently visit the Memorial during the Faith & Politics Institute's annual Civil Rights Pilgrimage to Alabama. Public education is one of the most important tools in the SPLC's efforts to fight hate and bigotry.

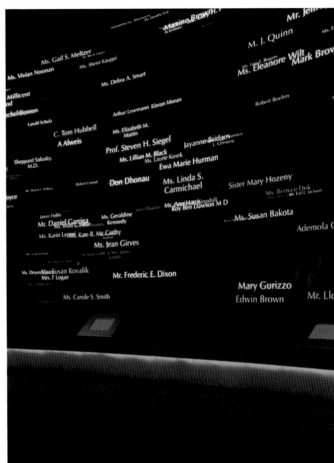

CIVIL RIGHTS MEMORIAL CENTER

In 2005, the SPLC opened the Civil Rights Memorial Center to deepen the educational experience of the Memorial. Tens of thousands of visitors—mostly schoolchildren— tour the interpretive center every year, introducing many to the story of the civil rights movement and the sacrifices that were made to win freedom for African Americans. Visitors can (from left) learn about the martyrs and take a virtual tour of other famous civil rights sites in Montgomery; view the film *Faces in the Water* in the Mike Stoller and Corky Hale Stoller Civil Rights Memorial Theater; learn about contemporary struggles in the march for justice; and pledge to stand against hate and injustice by signing the Wall of Tolerance, a digital display that now contains more than six hundred thousand names.

crimes against African Americans, LGBT people and other minorities. Dees believed the effort must begin with the nation's children. So the SPLC launched an investment in the future called Teaching Tolerance. The idea was to produce and distribute high-quality books, classroom films, lesson plans and other anti-bias materials that would help teachers promote respect and an appreciation of the nation's racial, ethnic and cultural diversity among their students—in short, to teach them tolerance before the seeds of hate could take root in their young hearts. Dees, having built a successful mail-order book-publishing business before founding the SPLC, had the expertise to make it work. And, because of the support of the SPLC's members, the organization was able to offer the materials to teachers for free.

The first issue of *Teaching Tolerance* magazine, filled with anti-bias lesson ideas and techniques teachers could use in their classrooms, was mailed to 150,000 teachers across the country in January 1992. It was an immediate hit. The SPLC followed up with the introduction of its first teaching kit—*America's Civil Rights Movement*—which contained the book *Free at Last* and a new film, *A Time for Justice*, produced by the SPLC and directed by Charles Guggenheim. Eighty thousand teachers sent in requests for the kit, and in 1995, the film won an Oscar for best short documentary.

Teaching Tolerance was off to a rousing start.

More film kits followed through the years. *Mighty Times: The Legacy of Rosa Parks* taught students about the Montgomery bus boycott and won an Emmy. *Mighty Times: The Children's March* told the story of the young people in Birmingham, Alabama, who brought segregation to its knees in that city. It won the SPLC its second Oscar in the short documentary category.

The SPLC partnered with the Gerda and Kurt Klein Foundation in 2005 to distribute the foundation's

Oscar-winning film *One Survivor Remembers*, which told the story of the Holocaust through the eyes of a girl, Gerda Klein, who lived through it. Another film kit, *Starting Small*, was designed for in-service training to help teachers learn classroom strategies to promote fairness, respect and tolerance.

In 2008, amid a divisive national debate over immigration—one punctuated by racism, distortions and false propaganda about Latinos—the SPLC produced a new film kit designed to illustrate the historic struggles faced by Latinos in America. *Viva La Causa* brought to life a seminal event in the march for human rights—the California grape strike and boycott led by labor organizers César Chávez and Dolores Huerta in the 1960s. It showed students how thousands of Americans across the country joined in a battle to improve the lives of some of the most exploited people in the country, the farmworkers who labored for meager wages under appalling conditions in the vineyards of California. It reminded students that they, too, had the power to change the world.

The SPLC premiered *Viva La Causa* before fifteen hundred people at the historic Wilshire Theater in Beverly Hills on September 28, 2008. Dolores Huerta, who appeared in the documentary and was still politically active, was on hand, as were hundreds of students and farmworkers and numerous SPLC supporters who had helped make the film possible with their donations.

"This film teaches me to never give up," said one Los Angeles-area student who attended the premiere. "It motivates me to fight for what is right." Another student added, "People need to know about this struggle. We hear little of it in school. I learned more about the farmworkers watching this film than I have in all my years of schooling."

Two years later, the SPLC released another classroom film with a social message that was particularly relevant at the time—*Bullied: A Student, a School and*

THE UNSOLVED MURDERS

When the Civil Rights Memorial was unveiled in 1989, the dedication was tinged with sadness because, in most cases, the families of the martyrs named on the granite table still waited for the killers to be brought to justice. At the time of the murders, local law enforcement and juries typically looked the other way, even when the killers' identities were known. But the Memorial helped spark renewed interest in solving the civil rights cold cases—and, in the aftermath, eight white supremacists were convicted for murdering thirteen of the martyrs.

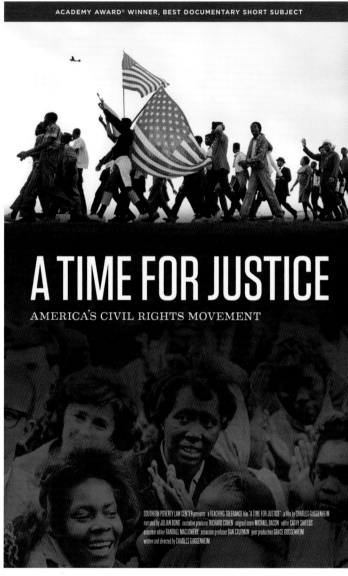

TEACHING
TOLERANCE

Spring/'92

AWARDED FOR EXCELLENCE
Morris Dees and filmmaker Charles Guggenheim pose in 1995 with the SPLC's first Academy Award—for *A Time for Justice*, a classroom documentary that captured the spirit of the civil rights movement through historical footage and the voices of those who participated in the struggle. SPLC President Richard Cohen served as executive producer of the film. Teaching Tolerance's anti-bias education materials, including its magazine, are sent free to hundreds of thousands of educators every year.

a Case that Made History. Across the country, stories of suicides by LGBT students who had been harassed by their classmates were making headlines. And in many schools, teachers and administrators were unwilling or afraid to openly address the problem. *Bullied* recounted the story of one student's lawsuit and a landmark court ruling holding public schools accountable for failing to protect LGBT students. It encouraged students to stand up for classmates who were being harassed, and it helped hundreds of thousands of school officials create safer environments for all students. The SPLC hosted screenings across the country for parent groups and others, and has distributed more than one hundred thousand copies since its release.

Publishing anti-bias materials was just one of Teaching Tolerance's strategies. In 2001, it created a program that breaks down social barriers, called Mix It Up at Lunch Day. The concept was simple. Research showed that the cafeteria was the place in school where student divisions were most clear. Studies also showed that biases and misconceptions tended to melt away when students interacted with others from different racial, social or cultural backgrounds. On Mix It Up Day, held in the fall each year, schools asked students to sit with someone new in the cafeteria. Thousands of schools across the country signed up to participate every year, and the SPLC provided free materials and activities that could be tailored to each school. Many teachers designed their own lesson plans around the concept and used the event to kick off year-long activities throughout their schools. The event reached thousands of schools and millions of students annually.

While reducing bias and creating safe learning environments for all students might seem to be universally supported goals, Teaching Tolerance's efforts were not without controversy. For example, several weeks before the 2012 Mix It Up at Lunch Day, the American

Family Association (AFA) sent out an email alert to its supporters urging them to contact local schools and demand they not participate in the event. Two years earlier, the SPLC had added the Tupelo, Mississippi-based organization to its list of hate groups.

What landed the AFA—which boasted of two million online supporters and broadcasts on two hundred radio stations—on the list was its endless use of false propaganda to demonize LGBT people. Its chief spokesman and radio host, Bryan Fischer had repeatedly linked gay men with the Holocaust.

"Homosexuality," Fischer wrote, "gave us Adolph Hitler, and homosexuals in the military gave us the Brown Shirts, the Nazi war machine and 6 million dead Jews." He also regularly—and falsely—equated gay men with pedophiles, even though the American Psychological Association had concluded that gay men were no more likely to molest children than were heterosexual men.

Under the headline "Radical Southern Poverty Law Center behind gay indoctrination program," the AFA told its supporters that Mix It Up Day was a "nationwide push to promote the homosexual lifestyle in public schools" and that the SPLC was trying to "intimidate and silence students who have a Biblical view of homosexuality."

Teaching Tolerance Director Maureen Costello told *The New York Times* she was "not surprised that they completely lied about what Mix It Up Day is. It was a cynical, fear-mongering tactic." The battle of words moved from the pages of the *Times* to CNN, where host Carol Costello (no relation) interviewed Fischer and ridiculed his claims.

It got worse for Fischer when he was lampooned by the host of *The Colbert Report*. "Don't fall for it kids," Stephen Colbert deadpanned. "It's a devious plot: Get kids to learn that despite our outward differences, in our hearts we're all pretty much the same."

CONTINUED ON **PAGE 218**

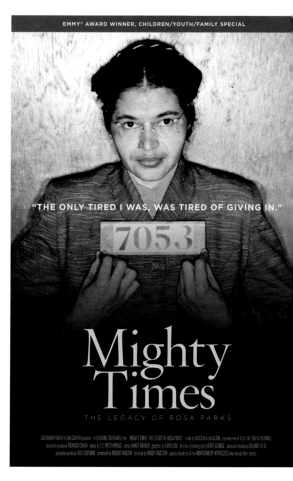

AWARD-WINNING DOCUMENTARIES

Since the early 1990s, Teaching Tolerance has equipped hundreds of thousands of educators with film-based teaching kits that reduce prejudice, improve intergroup relations and foster school equity. At left, SPLC President Richard Cohen (center) celebrates an Academy Award with directors Robert Hudson (left) and Bobby Houston. Original short documentaries produced by the SPLC have been recognized with numerous awards, including two Oscars—for *America's Civil Rights Movement: A Time for Justice* (1994) and *Mighty Times: The Children's March* (2004)—and an Emmy for *Mighty Times: The Legacy of Rosa Parks* (2005). Teaching kits are sent free to classroom teachers, librarians, school counselors, school administrators, professors of education, and others.

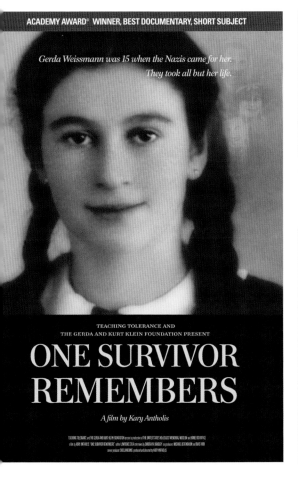

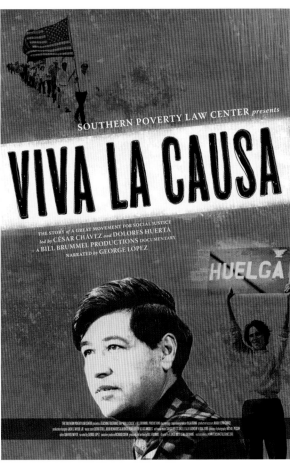

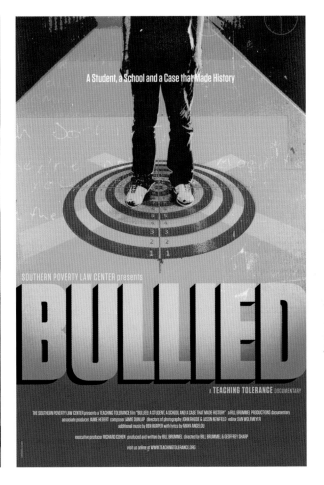

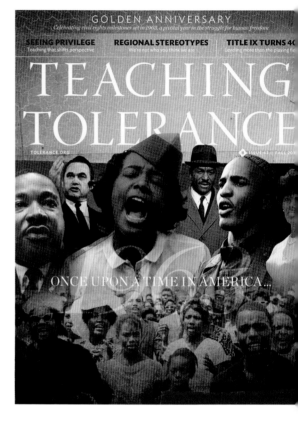

TEACHING TOLERANCE MAGAZINE

Teaching Tolerance helps educators create nurturing classrooms where the ideals of justice and equality are not only taught but lived. It contains lesson plans, articles and classroom exercises on social justice topics like LGBT bullying, civil rights education, and racial and gender equality. The publication—delivered to 450,000 educators twice each year, free of charge— has garnered more than twenty honors from the Association of Educational Publishers. In 2009, the AEP named *Teaching Tolerance* its Periodical of the Year.

Some schools did cancel their plans for Mix It Up Day, but the vast majority rejected the group's bigotry and fraudulent claims and conducted their plans as usual. In the end, the AFA's smear attempt succeeded merely in calling positive attention to the SPLC's efforts to fight prejudice.

Indeed, the continuing support for Teaching Tolerance was proof that it had become a trusted resource for teachers across the country. The recipient of numerous awards, the program had been named a "Friend of the U.N." and selected by President Bill Clinton's Initiative on Race as one of the nation's "Promising Practices" in the effort to eradicate racism.

Since the early 1990s, the SPLC had distributed more than 1.3 million teaching kits that cost a total of more than $12 million to produce. And each issue of its magazine was reaching 450,000 educators every year, with every school in the country receiving at least two copies. More than 90 percent of the teachers who used Teaching Tolerance resource``s and responded to a survey said they made a difference in their classrooms.

IN APRIL 2011, the SPLC celebrated forty years of fighting hate, seeking justice and teaching tolerance. More than fifteen hundred passionate supporters traveled to Montgomery, some from as far away as Hawaii and Alaska, to spend two days mingling with the founders, Morris Dees and Joe Levin, and the many others at the SPLC who helped forge a more just nation. They packed into churches and other venues to learn about the organization's landmark achievements. They exchanged ideas with SPLC lawyers on the cutting edge of social justice litigation. They sat in reverence in the pews of the Dexter Avenue King Memorial Baptist Church, where Dr. King preached in the 1950s and helped lead the Montgomery bus boycott. They spoke with civil rights icons like Julian

Bond, the SPLC's first president. And they shared moments of laughter and tears, a community of people united in their commitment to the ideals of equality and justice and dedicated to pursuing those ideals in their own lives.

They were people like Evelyn Green-Frierson—a descendant of abolitionist Harriet Tubman. "It is very disturbing that we live in a country today where we have freedom but still there are individuals [and] hate groups that are trying to hold different groups back because of race, because of class, because of gender," Green-Frierson said. "So we need organizations like the Southern Poverty Law Center to fight for our cause and to continue the cause that Dr. Martin Luther King had fought for so long—for us to have freedom."

They were people like Jim Fisher of Chicago, who said he was particularly upset that more than two years into President Obama's presidency, the nation's first black president still felt the need to produce a birth certificate to prove his legitimacy to hold office. "I'm very saddened by it and that's one of the many reasons I'm here," he said. "I just feel it's necessary to stand up."

And they were people like Bill Norton and his daughter, Therese, who traveled from Seattle as a way to celebrate her passing the bar exam, a milestone in a future law career inspired by a passion for social justice. "As far as I'm concerned, this is the premier legal-oriented organization in the country for social justice," Norton said.

As the celebration began, SPLC staffers gathered for a special anniversary greeting from a class of second graders at Notre Dame Elementary in Portsmouth, Ohio. With the help of an Internet video connection, the students told of actions they were taking to make the world a better place. The children sang "It Could be a Wonderful World" from Teaching

CONTINUED ON **PAGE 227**

MIX IT UP AT LUNCH
Mix It Up at Lunch Day, sponsored by Teaching Tolerance, encourages students to do something simple yet powerful— sit next to someone new in the cafeteria. Thousands of schools participate in the annual event. Studies have shown that when students interact with those who are different from them, biases and misperceptions tend to melt away.

SEEKING GENERATIONAL CHANGE

Thousands of students in schools across America participate in the annual Mix it Up at Lunch Day—a day when Teaching Tolerance asks students to move out of their comfort zones and connect with someone new over lunch. Students have identified the cafeteria as the place where social divisions are most clearly drawn in school. Mixing it up is a simple act with profound implications. Many schools create their own activities for the day and even have yearlong programs. Teaching Tolerance offers an array of free online resources designed to help school groups and classroom teachers explore the issue of social boundaries.

SPLC LEADERS CELEBRATE FOUR DECADES
As the SPLC in 2011 marked forty years of fighting hate and
seeking justice for society's most vulnerable, SPLC leaders
posed in front of the Civil Rights Memorial. From left: co-founder
Morris Dees, Civil Rights Memorial Center Director Lecia Brooks,
President Richard Cohen, SPLC's first president, Julian Bond, and
co-founder Joe Levin.

CELEBRATING FORTY YEARS

Julian Bond (far left) and SPLC President Richard Cohen (second from left) greet members during the SPLC's fortieth anniversary celebration. The three-day event in April 2011 brought more than a thousand supporters from around the country to Montgomery, Alabama, the birthplace of the civil rights movement. They enjoyed mingling with SPLC staff members—including Joe Levin (middle) and Morris Dees (right)—between lectures, Teaching Tolerance film screenings, panel discussions, and other events that focused on the SPLC's past, present and future.

Tolerance's music project "I Will Be Your Friend: Songs and Activities for Young Peacemakers."

Their teacher, Wanda Dengel, added, "We are so proud of all that you have done, not only in the vein of law but all the wonderful educational materials that you produce for all of us teachers all across America. Those materials have helped us to create young peacemakers not only in our classrooms but in our schools, our families and our communities all across America."

DURING ITS FIRST FOUR DECADES, the SPLC had shut down some of the nation's most dangerous white supremacist groups. It had attacked institutional racism in the South; reformed juvenile justice practices; shattered barriers to equality for women, children and the disabled; and protected low-wage immigrant workers from abuse. It had reached out to the next generation with Teaching Tolerance.

Its landmark legal work was part of a promise Dees and Levin made to their earliest supporters in 1971: They would bring cases that transform society.

"I like to think that when we made that commitment so long ago—and repeatedly over these last four decades—that we not only met your expectations but exceeded them," Levin told supporters. "What's happened has certainly exceeded mine."

Speaking to a crowd of more than one thousand seated in front of the Civil Rights Memorial, Dees reflected on the organization's success.

"Never would I have dreamed, nor would Joe Levin behind me have dreamed, when we started the Southern Poverty Law Center in a small office down the street—the two of us and a secretary—that I'd be standing here today in front of this magnificent structure with programs that reach all across the United States and the world, with you sitting here who have all made it possible," Dees said. "Thank you so very much."

Richard Cohen, the lawyer who had stood at Dees' side in the courtroom for twenty-five years, through many cases against violent racists, and been named SPLC president in 2003, spoke of the challenges ahead in a country where rapidly changing demographics were fueling xenophobia, hate and discrimination. He issued a pledge that echoed King's famous paraphrase of Amos 5:24, which is etched in the black granite of the Civil Rights Memorial:

"I promise you that when people cross that line between hate and hurt, when there are people out there who have no other champions, we will be there for them. And no matter what the risk to Morris—no matter what the risk to any of us—with your help, standing together, we will be there *until justice rolls down like waters and righteousness like a mighty stream.*" •

KEEPING THE DREAM ALIVE
The Civil Rights Memorial at the SPLC's main office stands as a constant reminder that the fight against hate and discrimination must continue, as Dr. Martin Luther King Jr. said, "until justice rolls down like waters and righteousness like a mighty stream."

REMEMBERING THE MARTYRS

FORTY NAMES ARE ETCHED INTO THE CIVIL RIGHTS MEMORIAL. Some were murdered because of their activism; others were victims of terror whose deaths propelled the movement by demonstrating the brutality faced by African Americans in the Jim Crow South. They included students, farmers, ministers, truck drivers, a homemaker, a deputy sheriff and a Nobel laureate. They ranged in age from 11 to 66. Thirty-two were black; eight were white. Below is a chronology of their deaths and other major events of the movement.

1954
May 17: Supreme Court outlaws school segregation in *Brown v. Board of Education*.

1955
May 7 · Belzoni, Mississippi

Rev. George Lee, one of the first black people registered to vote in Humphreys County, uses his pulpit and his printing press to urge others to vote. White officials offer him protection on the condition he end his voter registration efforts, but Lee refuses and is murdered.

August 13 · Brookhaven, Mississippi

Lamar Smith is shot dead on the courthouse lawn by a white man in broad daylight while dozens of people watch. The killer is never indicted because no one will admit they saw a white man shoot a black man. Smith had organized blacks to vote in a recent election.

August 28 · Money, Mississippi

Emmett Louis Till, a 14-year-old boy on vacation from Chicago, reportedly flirts with a white woman in a store. Three nights later, two men take Till from his bed, beat him, shoot him and dump his body in the Tallahatchie River. An all-white jury finds the men innocent of murder.

October 22 · Mayflower, Texas

John Earl Reese, 16, is dancing in a café when white men fire shots into the windows. Reese is killed and two others are wounded. The shootings are part of an attempt by whites to terrorize blacks into giving up plans for a new school. *(photograph unavailable)*

December 1 · Montgomery, Alabama
Rosa Parks is arrested for refusing to give up her seat on a bus to a white man.

December 5: Montgomery bus boycott begins.

1956
November 13: Supreme Court bans segregated seating on Montgomery buses.

1957
January 23 · Montgomery, Alabama

Willie Edwards Jr., a truck driver, is on his way to work when he is stopped by four Klansmen who mistake him for another man they believe is dating a white woman. Holding him at gunpoint, they force Edwards to jump off a bridge into the Alabama River. Edwards' body is found three months later.

August 29: Congress passes first Civil Rights Act since Reconstruction.

September 24 · Little Rock, Arkansas
President Eisenhower orders federal troops to enforce school desegregation.

1959
April 25 · Poplarville, Mississippi

Mack Charles Parker, 23, is accused of raping a white woman. Three days before his case is set for trial, a masked mob takes him from his jail cell, beats him, shoots him and throws him into the Pearl River.

1960
February 1 · Greensboro, North Carolina
Black students stage sit-in at "whites only" lunch counter.

December 5: Supreme Court outlaws segregation in bus terminals.

1961
May 14: Freedom Riders are attacked in Alabama while testing compliance with bus desegregation laws.

September 25 · Liberty, Mississippi

Herbert Lee, who worked with civil rights leader Bob Moses to help register black voters, is killed by a state legislator who claims self-defense and is never arrested. Louis Allen, a black man who witnesses the murder, is later also killed.

1962

April 1: Civil rights groups join forces to launch voter registration drive.

April 9 · Taylorsville, Mississippi

Cpl. Roman Ducksworth Jr., a military police officer stationed in Maryland, is on leave to visit his sick wife when he is ordered off a bus by a police officer and shot dead.

September 30: Riots erupt when James Meredith, a black student, enrolls at the University of Mississippi.

September 30 · Oxford, Mississippi

Paul Guihard, a reporter for a French news service, is killed by gunfire from a white mob during protests over the admission of James Meredith to the University of Mississippi.

1963

April 23 · Attalla, Alabama

William Lewis Moore, a postman from Baltimore, is shot and killed during a one-man march against segregation. Moore had planned to deliver a letter to the governor of Mississippi urging an end to intolerance.

May 3 · Birmingham, Alabama
Birmingham police attack marching children with dogs and firehoses

June 11: Alabama governor stands in schoolhouse door to stop integration at the University of Alabama.

June 12 · Jackson, Mississippi

Medgar Evers, who directed NAACP operations in Mississippi, is leading a campaign for integration in Jackson when he is shot and killed by a sniper at his home.

August 28 · Washington D.C.
250,000 Americans march on Washington for civil rights.

September 15 · Birmingham, Alabama

Addie Mae Collins, Cynthia Wesley, Denise McNair and **Carole Robertson** are getting ready for church services when a bomb explodes at the 16th Street Baptist Church, killing all four of the school-age girls. The church had been a center for civil rights meetings and marches.

September 15 · Birmingham, Alabama

Virgil Lamar Ware, 13, is riding on the handlebars of his brother's bicycle when he is fatally shot by white teenagers. The white youths had come from a segregationist rally held in the aftermath of the 16th Street Baptist Church bombing.

1964

January 23: Poll tax is outlawed in federal elections.

January 31 · Liberty, Mississippi

Louis Allen, who witnessed the murder of civil rights worker Herbert Lee, endured years of threats, jailings and harassment. He is making final arrangements to move north on the day he is killed.

April 7 · Cleveland, Ohio

Rev. Bruce Klunder is among civil rights activists protesting the building of a segregated school by placing their bodies in the way of construction equipment. Klunder is crushed to death when a bulldozer backs over him.

May 2 · Meadville, Mississippi

Henry Hezekiah Dee and **Charles Eddie Moore** are killed by Klansmen who believe the two are part of a plot to arm African Americans in the area. (There was no such plot.) Their bodies are found during a massive search for missing civil rights workers Chaney, Goodman and Schwerner.

June 20: Freedom Summer brings 1,000 young civil rights volunteers to Mississippi.

June 21 · Philadelphia, Mississippi

James Earl Chaney, **Andrew Goodman**, and **Michael Henry Schwerner**, young civil rights workers, are arrested by a deputy sheriff and then released into the hands of Klansmen. They are shot and buried in an earthen dam.

July 2: President Johnson signs Civil Rights Act of 1964.

July 11 · Colbert, Georgia

 Lt. Col. Lemuel Penn, a Washington, D.C., educator, is driving home from U.S. Army Reserve training when he is shot and killed by Klansmen in a passing car.

1965

February 26 · Marion, Alabama

 Jimmie Lee Jackson is beaten and shot by state troopers as he tries to protect his grandfather and mother from a trooper attack on civil rights marchers. His death leads to the Selma-to-Montgomery march and the eventual passage of the Voting Rights Act.

March 7 · Selma, Alabama
Now known as "Bloody Sunday," state troopers beat back peaceful marchers at Edmund Pettus Bridge.

March 11 · Selma, Alabama

 Rev. James Reeb, a Unitarian minister from Boston, is among many white clergymen who join the Selma marchers after the attack by state troopers at the Edmund Pettus Bridge. Reeb is beaten to death by white men while he walks down a Selma street.

March 25: Thousands complete Selma-to-Montgomery voting rights march

March 25 · Selma Highway, Alabama

 Viola Gregg Liuzzo, a housewife and mother from Detroit, drives alone to Alabama to help with the Selma march after seeing televised reports of the attack at the Edmund Pettus Bridge. She is driving marchers back to Selma from Montgomery when she is shot and killed by a Klansmen in a passing car.

June 2 · Bogalusa, Louisiana

 Oneal Moore is one of two black deputies hired by white officials in an attempt to appease civil rights demands. Moore and his partner, Creed Rogers, are on patrol when they are blasted with gunfire from a passing car. Moore is killed and Rogers wounded.

July 9: Congress passes Voting Rights Act of 1965.

July 18 · Anniston, Alabama

 Willie Brewster is on his way home from work when he is shot and killed by white men. The men belonged to the National States Rights Party, a violent neo-Nazi group whose members had been involved in church bombings and murders of African Americans.

August 20 · Hayneville, Alabama

Jonathan Myrick Daniels, an Episcopal seminary student in Boston, comes to Alabama to help with black voter registration in Lowndes County. He is arrested at a demonstration, jailed in Hayneville and then suddenly released. Moments later, he is shot to death by a deputy sheriff.

1966

January 3 · Tuskegee, Alabama

Samuel Leamon Younge Jr., a student civil rights activist, is fatally shot by a white gas station owner following an argument over segregated restrooms.

January 10 · Hattiesburg, Mississippi

Vernon Ferdinand Dahmer, a wealthy businessman, offers to pay poll taxes for those who can't afford the fee required to vote. The night after a radio station broadcasts Dahmer's offer, his home is firebombed. Dahmer later dies from severe burns.

June 10 · Natchez, Mississippi

Ben Chester White, who had worked most of his life as a caretaker on a plantation, had no involvement in civil rights work. He is murdered by Klansmen in a plot to lure Dr. King to the town so they could assassinate him.

July 30 · Bogalusa, Louisiana

Clarence Triggs was a bricklayer who had attended civil rights meetings sponsored by the Congress of Racial Equality. He is found dead on a roadside, shot through the head. (*photograph unavailable*)

1967

February 27 · Natchez, Mississippi

Wharlest Jackson, the treasurer of his local NAACP chapter, is one of many African Americans who received threatening Klan notices at his job. After Jackson is promoted to a position previously reserved for whites, a bomb is planted in his car. It explodes minutes after he leaves work one day, killing him instantly.

May 12 · Jackson, Mississippi

Benjamin Brown, a former civil rights organizer, is watching a student protest from the sidelines when he is hit by stray gunshots from police who fire into the crowd.

October 2: Thurgood Marshall is sworn in as first black Supreme Court justice.

1968

February 8 · Orangeburg, South Carolina

Samuel Ephesians Hammond Jr., **Delano Herman Middleton** and **Henry Ezekial Smith** are shot and killed by police who fire on student demonstrators at the South Carolina State College campus.

April 4 · Memphis, Tennessee

Dr. Martin Luther King Jr., a Baptist minister and major architect of the civil rights movement, led and inspired non-violent campaigns, including those in Montgomery and Birmingham. He was awarded the Nobel Peace Prize. He is assassinated as he prepares to lead a demonstration in Memphis.

CHRONOLOGY

1970
A federal court rules the YMCA in Montgomery, Alabama, must end its policy of racial discrimination, in a case filed by Morris Dees.

1971
Morris Dees and Joe Levin formally incorporate the SPLC. Julian Bond is named as its first president.

1972
A federal court accepts an SPLC plan to reapportion the Alabama Legislature, ensuring equal representation for African Americans. Two years later, fifteen black lawmakers are elected; previously, only two had been elected since Reconstruction.

An SPLC suit forces the integration of the Alabama State Troopers, which had never had a black trooper. A federal judge orders the state to hire one black trooper for every white until the force is 25 percent African-American.

1973
The U.S. Supreme Court rules that dependents of servicewomen must receive the same benefits as those of servicemen, upholding the SPLC's victory in the first successful sex discrimination case against the federal government.

A federal court decree in an SPLC case guarantees African Americans access to the same funeral services at the same prices offered to whites.

1974
The SPLC secures an agreement with a state-licensed orphanage in Alabama to provide a home for orphaned and neglected black children, many of whom were previously sent to correctional institutions because no shelters would take them.

1975
The SPLC wins freedom for three African-American men—known as the Tarboro Three—who spent two years on North Carolina's death row after being wrongfully convicted of raping a white woman.

1976
A federal judge rules Alabama prisons are "wholly unfit for human habitation" in an SPLC case. SPLC lawyers work for more than a decade to force the state to bring the prisons up to constitutional standards.

1977
The U.S. Supreme Court, ruling in an SPLC case, opens the door for women to fill law enforcement jobs traditionally held by men.

1978
The federal government adopts new rules prohibiting the forced sterilization of poor women following an SPLC lawsuit filed on behalf of two African-American girls sterilized without their consent.

1979
A federal judge finds in an SPLC suit that the at-large system of electing city commissioners in Montgomery County, Alabama, illegally dilutes the voting power of African Americans; orders new plan based on single-member districts.

1980
Morris Dees files the SPLC's first case against a hate group, suing the Invisible Empire, Knights of the Ku Klux Klan after its members, armed with guns, ax handles and bats, attack peaceful civil rights marchers in Decatur, Alabama.

U.S. Supreme Court vacates the convictions of eleven death row inmates in Alabama after affirming the SPLC's claim that the state's death penalty statute is unconstitutional.

1981
A Klan terror campaign against Vietnamese fishermen on Galveston Bay in Texas is shut down by an SPLC lawsuit.

The SPLC creates Klanwatch to monitor Klan factions across the country. It is later renamed the Intelligence Project to reflect the broader mission of tracking many types of hate and extremist groups.

1982
The SPLC wins the release of Johnny Ross, a black teen who became the nation's youngest death row inmate at 16 after being wrongly convicted of raping a white woman in Louisiana in 1975.

1983
The SPLC's office is firebombed on July 28.

The SPLC wins settlement to compensate six Alabama textile mill workers who contracted brown lung disease.

1984
After a seventeen-month investigation by the SPLC and law enforcement, three Alabama Klansmen are arrested for setting fire to the SPLC office. All plead guilty and are sent to prison.

The SPLC's investigation into the attack on marchers in Decatur, Alabama, leads to indictments against nine Klansmen. Separately, a court orders the Invisible Empire, the Klan faction sued by the SPLC over the attack, to stop operating as a paramilitary force.

1985

An SPLC suit forces Glenn Miller's Carolina Knights of the Ku Klux Klan to cease paramilitary operations and stop harassing African Americans.

The SPLC moves into its new office in downtown Montgomery, Alabama.

1986

The SPLC presents evidence to the Pentagon that active-duty soldiers are engaged in paramilitary training with the White Patriot Party, a Klan group in North Carolina. Defense Secretary Caspar Weinberger issues a directive that personnel "must reject" participation in hate groups.

Acting as special U.S. prosecutors, Morris Dees and Richard Cohen help win a criminal contempt conviction against White Patriot Party leader Glenn Miller for violating a 1985 court order to stop paramilitary operations. Miller goes underground and calls for followers to kill Dees.

1987

The SPLC wins an historic $7 million verdict against the United Klans of America—a group responsible for some of the worst violence of the civil rights era—for the 1981 lynching of Michael Donald in Mobile, Alabama.

The U.S. Supreme Court upholds the SPLC's affirmative action plan for the Alabama State Troopers in the 1972 desegregation case.

1988

The SPLC wins nearly $1 million judgment against two Klan groups and eleven followers responsible for an attack on peaceful marchers in Forsyth County, Georgia. The Invisible Empire disbands after paying damages.

Klan leader Glenn Miller pleads guilty to charges related to his threats against Morris Dees. He serves three years in federal prison.

1989

The Civil Rights Memorial, sponsored by the SPLC and designed by Maya Lin, is dedicated at the SPLC office in Montgomery. The SPLC publishes *Free At Last*, which tells the stories of the forty martyrs whose names are inscribed on the Memorial.

The SPLC wins a settlement against the Invisible Empire for its bloody attack on peaceful civil rights marchers in Decatur, Alabama, a decade earlier. The Klansmen must attend a race relations course taught by leaders of the group they attacked.

The SPLC wins a financial settlement for the family of Loyal Garner, a black truck driver beaten to death by lawmen in an East Texas jail. SPLC evidence helps convict three officials of criminal charges.

1990

The SPLC wins a $12.5 million judgment against Tom and John Metzger and their hate group, White Aryan Resistance, for their role in the murder of Ethiopian graduate student Mulugeta Seraw by racist skinheads in Portland, Oregon.

The SPLC begins to track hate groups more closely by conducting an annual census and plotting their locations on a U.S. map.

1991

The SPLC launches Teaching Tolerance to combat prejudice by providing free anti-bias classroom materials to teachers across the nation.

Two hundred Klan members march on the SPLC office and the Civil Rights Memorial on March 9, carrying a banner that reads "Morris Dees—Enemy of the People."

The SPLC settles a major mental health lawsuit in Alabama, spurring dramatic changes in the way child welfare authorities provide for children with mental health needs.

1992

The SPLC distributes the first issue of *Teaching Tolerance* magazine to 150,000 teachers, and its first anti-bias teaching kit, *America's Civil Rights Movement*, which includes the classroom film *A Time for Justice*.

1993

An SPLC lawsuit forces the state of Alabama to remove the Confederate battle flag from atop the Capitol, where segregationist Governor George Wallace raised it in 1963 in defiance of federal efforts to integrate public schools.

1994

The SPLC wins $1 million judgment in case against the Church of the Creator after a member of the neo-Nazi group murders Harold Mansfield, an African-American sailor.

The SPLC launches an investigation of white supremacist activity within the antigovernment militia movement. Six months before the April 1995 Oklahoma City bombing, Morris Dees writes a letter warning U.S. Attorney General Janet Reno of the danger.

Teaching Tolerance's first classroom film, *A Time for Justice*, wins the Academy Award for Best Documentary (Short Subject).

1995

Indigent dialysis patients in Alabama receive state-funded transportation to medical treatments following an SPLC lawsuit.

1996

Alabama prisons are forced to abandon the use of chain gangs following an SPLC lawsuit.

The SPLC wins an $85,000 judgment against William Pierce, the neo-Nazi leader whose novel inspired the Oklahoma City bombing, after a jury finds he was involved in a scheme to hide assets of a hate group sued by the SPLC, the Church of the Creator.

Members of the Oklahoma Constitutional Militia are sentenced to prison in a plot to destroy the SPLC office with an ammonium nitrate bomb, the same kind used in the Oklahoma City bombing a year earlier.

The Teaching Tolerance film *The Shadow of Hate* is nominated for an Academy Award.

1997

A federal judge rules in an SPLC suit that Alabama's use of the "hitching post" on inmates violates the U.S. Constitution's ban on "cruel and unusual punishment." Inmates were shackled for hours in painful positions, often roasting in the hot sun.

1998

The SPLC wins the largest judgment ever against a hate group when a South Carolina jury orders the Christian Knights of the Ku Klux Klan and five Klansmen to pay $37.8 million (later reduced to $21.5 million) for conspiring to burn the Macedonia Baptist Church.

1999

Klansman Wallace Weicherding and New Order leader Dennis McGiffen are sent to prison for conspiracy in connection with a plot to kill Morris Dees by bombing the SPLC office.

2000

The SPLC secures a $6.3 million verdict against the Aryan Nations and its leader, Richard Butler, after the neo-Nazi group's members terrorize a mother and son. Butler must give up the twenty-acre Idaho compound that is home to the nation's most violent white supremacists.

Dramatic improvements are made in the health care received by Alabama's mentally ill inmates after a settlement is reached in an SPLC lawsuit.

2001

Klansman Jeff Berry is ordered to pay $120,000 in damages to two journalists held captive at his Indiana home in November 1999, in SPLC suit.

The SPLC moves into a new office building across the street from the Civil Rights Memorial and its old office.

2002

Teaching Tolerance launches the annual Mix It Up at Lunch Day, a program that encourages schoolchildren to cross social and racial boundaries.

2003

Winning a lawsuit against Alabama Chief Justice Roy Moore to enforce the constitutional separation of church and state, the SPLC forces the removal of a Ten Commandments monument from the state Supreme Court building.

Richard Cohen is named SPLC president, seventeen years after joining the organization as its legal director.

2004

The SPLC launches its Immigrant Justice Project to address the exploitation of vulnerable immigrants.

The SPLC exposes and helps stop stealth efforts by anti-immigrant activists to seize control of the Sierra Club.

An SPLC suit forces Alabama's prison system to provide adequate health care to inmates with chronic illnesses.

The Teaching Tolerance production *Mighty Times: The Children's March* wins the Oscar, the SPLC's second for Best Documentary (Short Subject).

2005

The SPLC wins more than $1 million in settlements and judgments in case against the border vigilante group Ranch Rescue after two Salvadoran immigrants are assaulted, terrorized and falsely imprisoned in Texas.

The Teaching Tolerance film *Mighty Times: The Legacy of Rosa Parks* wins a Daytime Emmy.

The SPLC opens the Civil Rights Memorial Center in its former office. Thousands attend the Oct. 23 ceremony.

2006

Mississippi enacts legislation, developed with the SPLC, that radically overhauls the state's juvenile justice system to reduce the incarceration of nonviolent children and teens.

An SPLC suit wins settlement worth up to $1 million for migrant workers who were cheated out of wages after working to clean up New Orleans in the aftermath of Hurricane Katrina.

2007

A Texas jury awards $9 million to Billy Ray Johnson, a black man with mental disabilities who was beaten and dumped along a road by four white men in 2003. The SPLC filed suit after the men received jail sentences of thirty to sixty days.

The SPLC assists the U.S. Justice Department in reopening civil rights-era cold cases.

2008

The SPLC wins $2.5 million judgment against the leader of the Imperial Klans of America and several members after Klansmen savagely beat a teenage boy of Panamanian descent at a county fair in Kentucky.

The state of Mississippi closes its Columbia Training School, a prison for girls, seven months after the SPLC sues to stop the physical and sexual abuse of teenage girls confined there.

The SPLC exposes John Tanton, the architect of the anti-immigrant movement, as a key player in the white nationalist world.

2009

The Pentagon tightens its policy banning white supremacist or extremist activity in the military after the SPLC uncovers neo-Nazis among active-duty personnel.

The SPLC exposes a powerful resurgence of the antigovernment militia movement, driven in part by the election of the nation's first black president.

2010

Superior Forestry Service agrees to pay $2.75 million to settle an SPLC lawsuit filed on behalf of guest workers who were systematically cheated out of wages by the Arkansas company. The settlement is among the largest of its kind.

The town of Homer, Louisiana, settles an SPLC lawsuit on behalf of the widow of an elderly black man shot to death on his front porch by a white police officer in 2009.

The SPLC wins a settlement for farmworkers who were cheated out of wages while working in the onion fields of South Georgia for a subsidiary of Del Monte.

2011

SPLC reaches a settlement with Candy Brand, which agrees to pay $1.5 million in back wages to 1,500 guest workers who harvested and packed tomatoes for the Arkansas company.

More than 1,500 SPLC supporters gather at the Montgomery office to celebrate the organization's 40th anniversary and look ahead to the challenges of the future.

2012

Responding to an SPLC lawsuit, federal courts block most provisions of Alabama's harsh anti-immigrant law. The U.S. Supreme Court later refuses to hear Alabama's appeal and a final settlement places additional limits on racial profiling under the law

In a groundbreaking settlement, the state of Mississippi is required to remove children and teens from the adult population of a for-profit prison, protect them from violence and sexual abuse, and provide adequate rehabilitative services.

Minnesota's largest school district agrees to protect LGBT students from abuse to settle an SPLC suit filed to address rampant anti-LGBT violence and harassment following multiple student suicides related to bullying.

The American Bar Association bestows its highest honor, the ABA Medal, upon Morris Dees for a legal career dedicated to seeking justice and equality.

A federal court orders Eller and Sons Trees Inc. to pay $11.8 million to 4,000 foreign guest workers cheated out of wages while employed by the Georgia forestry company—the largest court award to date on behalf of guest workers.

A jury orders a labor recruiting firm and its owner to pay $4.5 million to 350 Filipino teachers represented by the SPLC. The teachers were forced into exploitive contracts after being lured to teach in Louisiana public schools as guest workers.

The SPLC files a first-of-its-kind lawsuit accusing a New Jersey organization of consumer fraud for offering "conversion therapy," a discredited practice purporting to convert LGBT people to straight.

2013

In a historic ruling secured by the SPLC, a federal court finds that a law preventing veterans in same-sex marriages from receiving equal benefits from the U.S. Department of Veterans Affairs is unconstitutional.

An SPLC lawsuit challenging Georgia's anti-immigrant law concludes after it successfully blocks several provisions of the draconian law.

2014

The SPLC sues the state of Tennessee for practices that block thousands of low-income residents from receiving Medicaid despite their eligibility.

THE MORRIS DEES LEGACY FUND

THE SOUTHERN POVERTY LAW CENTER extends its gratitude to the following members who have generously contributed to the Morris Dees Legacy Fund. The SPLC is supported primarily through private donations; it neither accepts government funds nor takes any part of the recoveries it secures for its clients. The Morris Dees Legacy Fund will help ensure that the SPLC's work for justice and equality continues far into the future.

FOUNDERS' CIRCLE

William E. Little Jr. and Family
Barbara J. Meislin — The Purple Lady
David and Cecile Wang
Dr. Jane L. Winer and Dr. Monty J. Strauss

PRESIDENT'S CIRCLE

Stephen D. Senturia

LEADERS CIRCLE

Orrie M. and Laurel E. Friedman
Joseph F. McCrindle Foundation
James "Mac" McElroy
Helen and Oliver Wolcott and Family

CHAMPIONS CIRCLE

Robert Ayers
Burt and Diana Cutler Family Foundation
Ferguson Foundation
Edward and Alma Greer
Herbert M. Citrin Charitable Foundation
Marilyn and James Heskett
Linda Look
Kurt and Therese Melden
Melvin S. and Corinne Moss of Blessed Memory
Lida Orzeck, PhD
Jeffrey and Valerie Paley Family
Charles A. Ranney
In Memory of Gerald M. Surette
Susan F. Tobin
Cynthia Perrine Wilcox
Willow Springs Foundation

ADVOCATES CIRCLE

Full Circle Foundation
Gina Harman Foundation
Todd and Lorella Hess
Anita Hirsh
Martin and Marci Karplus
Gregory Lincoln
Edith MacGuire
Pettit Foundation
Kenneth and Colleen Rand
Happy and Bill Rands
S. Herbert Rubin
Carol G. Walter

MARCHERS CIRCLE

Judith W. Bruce
Nancy Joy Corcoran-Gordon
Peggy Cowles
Sandra Davidson
Drs. Andrew G. Dean and Consuelo M. Beck-Sague,
    Jeffrey A. Dean and Heidi Hopper
James and Lionelle Elsesser
The Gessner-Nelson Family
Marcy and Bennett Grau
Patty and Jeff Horing
Karuna Foundation,
    In Memory of Ron Maynard
Charley Kearns and Frank Ching
Nena P. Donovan Levine,
    In Memory of Louise Priddie Donovan
J Kent and Mary Nan McHose
In Memory of Helen Moore

Elisa Moran and Gary Kleiman
Nancy Newbury-Andresen
Joyce I. Nies and Peter A. Witt
Ellen Nusblatt
June Miller Rosenblatt
Elayne and Bill Roskin
Arnold Shapiro and Karen MacKain
Jeanne and Stuart Smolkin,
    In Honor of Mollye and William Smolkin
Elizabeth Steele
Ann P. and John E. Such
Angela Summers and Sanjeev Lahoti
Norman and Barbara Tanner
Gerald and Ruth Vurek
Howard, Jana and Ari Wolff

DIAMOND CIRCLE

Ann and Jules Gottlieb Foundation
Bob and Kathy Becker,
    Horncrest Foundation
Russ and Cordy Beckstead
Henry and Rhoda Bernstein
Alison Bronstein
Kicab Castaneda-Mendez and Marta Chase
Cynthia C. Cook
Ethan and Nancy Cutts
In Memory of Charlotte Dutka
Ms. Sandra Esner
Marietta Ethier and John McGarry
E. Ann Francis
Harold W. Ritchey Family Foundation
Julie H. Hoover

Glen D. Hunt

Nora Taylor Jaffe

Joseph W. Cotchett Foundation

Florence Koplow

Dr. and Mrs. Kenneth S. Kamer

Lou Kling

Nettie Kravitz

Ernest and Alisa Kretzmer

In Memory of Robert Thaddeus Lash

Maxwell Strawbridge Foundation

Dr. Matilda B. Melnick

Ann S. Merritt

Ronald R. and Wanda J. Mourant

Leslie Oelsner

David R. Owens and Dennis E. Morin,
    In Memory of Rita J. Morin

Diane Williams Parker

Linda Shiflet Pillow

Priscilla Endicott Charitable Foundation

Ronus Foundation

Alice and Thomas Schelling

Diane H. Schetky, MD

Charles E. Shepard

Gen. and Mrs. W. Y. Smith,
    Frank and Janina Petschek Foundation

Shirley Solomon

Dr. George Thoma

Wolfen Family Foundation

Xerox Foundation

PLATINUM CIRCLE

Audrey and Sargent Aborn

Alex Volkhausen and Tiger Baron Foundation

Ann and Jules Gottlieb Foundation

H. Brent and Joanne P. Austin

Mr. Alan G. Blush

Dr. and Mrs. Robert C. Bolz

Rena Bransten

Carl Jacobs Foundation

Donna L. Courtney

Kelly K. Curtis, MD

Mary Dresser

E. Bryce and Harriet Alpern Foundation

Mr. Donald T. Ferron

Lucy J. Hadac

Dr. Freda Lewis-Hall and Emerson Randy Hall Jr.

David and Carolyn Hinderliter

Priscilla S. Hunt

Elizabeth Judge

Kind World Foundation

Ms. Jeanne Learman

Emanuel Levy

Samuel Lionel

Lowitz Foundation

Roslyn Mandel

Mandell and Madeleine Berman Foundation

Manny and Ruthy Cohen Foundation

John and Linda Mason

Ben and Gwen Mirtz

M.J. and Caral G. Lebworth Foundation

Dr. Diana F. Nelson

William and Molly Norwood

Nonna Noto

Larry and Joy O'Rourke

Patti and Bob Plitt

Reginald F. Lewis Foundation

Michael Rosenbaum and Jill Rosenbaum

Carrie Shepard

Sinsinawa Dominican Congregation

Slomo and Cindy Silvian Foundation

Dr. Alexis Strongin and Mr. Steven Strongin

Mary Wall

The Rev. Ann Walling

William P. Goldman and Brothers Foundation

In Memory of Charles R. Zweizig Jr.

GOLD CIRCLE

Ms. Barbara Abruzzo and Ms. Connie Schofield

Robert J. Awkward

An Bergo and Gil Eisner

Celeste Birkhofer, PhD

Nellie C. Blackwell

Mrs. Anne C. Britt

Prof. Art Campfield

Louise Britt Carvey

Yvonne F. Clement

Mr. and Mrs. Lester Cohen

Dr. Seymour I. Cohen

Anne S. Covert

Crow Farm Foundation

Elaine S. Cummings

Daniel Nir and Jill Braufman Family Foundation

James K. DiCarlo

E.F. Harris Family Foundation

Mr. Dennis Egre

Dorothy Eley

Judy Faitek

Gay A. Fischer

David L. Forbes

Ms. Sarajane Foster

Dermot Frengley

Barbara G. Gottlieb

Pia and Rolf Habersang

Dr. Willis D. Hawley

Dr. Donald M. Hayes

Highland Mills Foundation

Mr. Peter Hoffenberg,
  Sidney Stern Memorial Trust

Mr. Dennis A. Hunter and Ms. Jill S. Hunter

Dr. Lenore Jacoby

Mr. Daniel Jantsch and Mrs. Thomas Jantsch

Patricia A. Jones

Carelle L. Karimimanesh and Mahmood K. Manesh

Ms. Ardith Kerst,
  Briggs-Kerst Family Foundation

Dag Knudsen

Mr. Paul LeFort and Mrs. Eileen LeFort

Mrs. Lois K. Lighthart

James and Susan Lowell

Ms. Irma J. Lunderman and Mr. William Lunderman

Dorothy Lurie, PhD and Greg Cantrell

Anne H. Martyn, PhD

McKibben Merner Family Foundation

Beitha Mendez

Frances Lee Meyer

Mr. Charles Richie Miller

Ms. Marianne Mitosinka and Mr. George Wick

Hetty Muller

Ann Noriega

Frances M. O'Hern

Lovell and Jack H. Olender,
  Olender Foundation

Mr. Stephen Ondra

Don Owens and Bess Owens

Shih Yuen Pai

Margaret P. Parker

Daniel K. Paulien

Pauline and Drew Pomerance

Constance and Bert Rabinowitz

Ms. Suzann Reynolds

Mrs. Concetta V. Ross

David Rothstein and Marcia Osburne

Samuel and Grace Gorlitz Foundation

Wesley N. Schulze

Mr. and Mrs. Gordon Segal

Ms. Meribeth Shank and Arden Shank

Rochelle and Gary Shelton

Ms. Joan M. Smith and Mr. Frank Smith

Charlotte Smith

Ms. Elaine Solley

C. Edward Spiegel

Elizabeth G. Stevens

Suzi and Dennis Strauch

Tartell Family Foundation

Dr. Reed Tuckson and Mrs. Margie Malone Tuckson

Jack and Blanche Valancy

M. Marie Waite

Bonnie Wilpon

SILVER CIRCLE

Neal B. Abraham and Ms. Donna L. Wiley

Drs. Taeko H. Ishida Abramson and Stanley R. Abramson

Ms. Jean Ackerman

Leticia A. Acosta

Stanley I. Adelstein and Hope S. Adelstein

Ruth and Ernest Adler

Alexander Family Charitable Giving Fund

Ms. Nancy O. Andrews and Ms. Amy Risch

Jane M. Anthony

Dawn Aoki

James Apone

Alan M. Appleford

Ms. Gloria Ayvazian

Dr. Earl Babbie and Mrs. Suzanne Babbie

Jon Baker and Marsha Baker

Charlotte Balfour

Mr. Howard Banchik

Ms. Minda F. Barnes

Shaleen C. Barnes

Susan and Barry Baskin

Richard A. Baumgartner

Mr. and Mrs. Seymour B. Bearak

B. Richard Benioff and Mary R. Benioff

Doris Bergen

Helen Berman

Dr. Leonard Bernstein and Dr. Jane Bernstein

John Biggs

Neil Blitstein and Chris Blitstein

Ms. Jane R. Brady

Mr. Arthur T. Brooks

Dr. Dorothy Lynn Brooks

Samuel and Roz Brott

Ms. Sharon E. Brown

Mr. Bunyan Bryant

Joanna Buck

Dr. John Buehler

Lucinda W. Bunnen

William A. Bush

Dr. Lynn Caporale

Dr. M. Olga Cardenas

Lois J. Carson

Dr. Jim Charles

Jeff and Karla Chaudoir

Theodore K. Cheng and Dr. Michelle Lee

Mr. Gordon Chin

Paul B. and Elizabeth M. Chmelik

Ms. Mary Christlieb

Theodore Chu

Jessica Clarke and Drew Coxhead

Clem C. Glass Foundation

Mr. Martin Cobin

Larry A. Cole and Cathy J. Cole

Henry A. Coleman, PhD

Ms. Marcie Colpas

Ana Alvarez Conigliaro

Richard and Barbara Conklin

Joan Cooper

Mary T. Cooper

Peter Cory and Maxine Creanza

Martha Clayton Cottrell, MD,
    In Honor of Charles Tillman Clayton

Mr. Leslie H. Cox

Ms. Nancy R. Crow and Mr. Mark A.A. Skrotzki

Douglas Daetz and Gisela Daetz

Anne Dahling

Will Dann and Melanie Cahn Dann

Ms. Betsy Darken

Jacqueline Davis and Jack Glickman

Susan Day

Mrs. Mary Lou DeFilippo

Logan S. Deimler

In Memory of Charles DeMarzo

Julett Denton

Mr. Frank R. Desantis

Ms. Theresa G. Destito

Mrs. Elinor Deutsch

Mildred L. Dold

Juliane M. Dow

Ms. Dorothy E. Downey

Dr. Joel Edelstein, Elizabeth McKinstry and Arin Edelstein

Elizabeth MacColl Charitable Fund

John Norig Ellison

C.R. Enever

Mary H. Epting

Donna and Hal Estry

Charlotte and Daniel Eth

Dr. Peter Facione and Dr. Noreen Facione

Michael S. Farber

Mick Favor

Mr. Thomas F. Fay

Harley Featherston

Dr. Micheline Federman

Ms. Kay Felt

Mr. John C. Fenoglio

Ferris and Salter, P.C.

Adrienne Fields

Ms. Judith Fiene

Dr. Thomas E. Finucane and Dr. Robin McKenzie

Bernice A. Fischer

Loyd K. Fischer and M. Marie Fischer

Leona Fisher

Eric L. Fitzpatrick

Michael T. Flora

Patricia L. Fluhrer, MD

Sheldon T. Fong

Wilmer Fong

Rita and Edward Forscher

Fortview Foundation

Karen Katayama Fox

Schley Franklin

Elaine C. Frederick

Thomas Freeman and Wendy-Sue Rosen

Mr. Hal Friedman

Mr. Benjamin Froman

Ms. Candus Fujiwara

Wendi and Michael Furman

Gina Gerwin Garnett

Ms. Paula Gaylord

Gershon (Gus) and Betty Carlson Gendler

Gertrude B. and Mortimer May Foundation

Mr. Frank Gibson and Maria Gibson

Kathy Gillespie and Debbie Epstein

Oscar A. Goldfarb

Prof. Thomas K. and Mrs. Marcia A. Goldstick

Mr. Daniel Goroff

Ralleigh Grandberry III

Mr. Ed Graves

Mr. Tom Gray

Rabbi Micah D. Greenstein and Sheril Greenstein

Mary W. Greenwald

Lumina Greenway

Sammye C. Greer

Mrs. Jenny Greyson

Linda J. Griffith and Scott K. Kellogg

Dr. Robert E. Grimes

Donita and Roy Gross

Ms. Shirley C. Hager

Jeffrey C. Hall

Dr. Thomas L. Hall and Ms. Elizabeth McLoughlin,
    Onward Fund

Marian Halley

Ann Halpern

Dr. Thomas E. Hamilton

Mr. Bernard Hammer

Mr. Michael A. Hamway

Ermaline T. Hannum

Ms. Bonnie Hano and Mr. Arnold Hano

Dr. William C. Haponski and Sandra G. Haponski

Ms. Marge Harburg

Tamara Harris and Reuben Harris

Dr. Joseph Hart and Mrs. Susan Hart

Carolyn Hartnett

Dr. Mary A. Hartshorn

Arthur J. Haskell

John H. Hatheway

Edward Hayes

Joseph R. Heller, PhD

Dr. and Mrs. Robert J. Heller and Debra Silver Heller

Sigrid Hepp-Dax

Pamela Kathleen Hill

Mr. Douglas Hillmer and Mrs. Karen Hillmer

Arline and Tom Hinckley

Susan J. Holliday

Elaine M. Hopson

Eloise W. Hunt

Rita Nartimatsu Inoway

Ms. Vera S. Irvin

Ms. Gail S. Isen and Charles Isen

Mr. and Mrs. Leighton T. Izu

Mr. Warren Jefferis

Ms. Lorraine Jensen

Ms. Mary R. Jewell

Mr. Sharad Jogal

Dr. Jesse P. Johnson

Joann and Kent Johnson

Dr. Leanor B. Johnson

Livingstone M. Johnson

Larry Jones

Mrs. Margaret L.C. Jones and Mr. William A. Jones Jr.

Dr. Floyd L. Judd

Prof. Judy M. Judd

Ms. Randy Kammer and Mr. Jeffry Wollitz

Bobbi Katz

Paul R. Kaup

Meridith E. Keating

Ms. Nancy Brown Keck

Ms. Maureen Kedes

Mr. Michael Keleher,
    Guadalupe Institute

Ms. Jeanie S. Kilgour and Mr. Murray S. Kilgour

Mr. Jon C. King

Douglas Kinney

Diana Klebanow

Ms. Patricia A. Klein and Mr. Daniel Snow

Hilda Knobloch, MD

Ida Kofsky

Ms. Judith Kostman and Mr. Charles Sternberg

Ms. Maggie Kotuk

Marcelline Krafchick

Mr. and Mrs. Lawrence Krasnow

Joan Kriikku

Ms. Elise Kroeber

Gael Kurath

Bill Lands

Mary E. Lane

Sally Leach

Emily Leff

Mr. Steven Leibler

Norma Leising

Melvin Levine

Beatrice R. Lewis

Mary R. Lewis, PhD

Dr. Ruth T. Lim

Philomena Lin and Matthew Chen

Gary Littlefield

Cecily D. Littleton

Mr. Jimmy Loyless and Elizabeth W. Loyless

Beth Luey and Michael Luey

Diana Fine Luks

Mr. Vincent N. Lunetta and Mrs. Lois W. Lunetta

Merle A. Lustig

Edith M. Lycke

Lawrence and Marianne Lynnworth

Patricia J. Lyon

Ms. Alice Lytle

Alex MacDonald II

Mr. D. Gordon MacLeod and Mrs. Susan H. Macleod

Mr. Brian Markey

Dr. Kimberly Marshall and Adam Zweiback

Maxine Martin

Mr. Joseph Mascarenhas

Christine Masters and Alan Ribakoff

Patricia C. Masterson

Becky Mathews

Claudette M. Mayer

Lavonne M. and Thomas G. McCombie Jr.

Mr. Ed McConnell

Jay A. and Janet S. McDonald

Anne McFarland

George W. McIntyre Jr.

Mr. Hugh S. McKenzie

Ms. Kathryn McLane and Mr. Mark McLane

Dr. Verne E. Mendel

Ms. Deena Mersky

Pamela J. Meyer

Mrs. Eleanor Meyerhoff

Judith G. Mich

Joan Millea

Ms. Julie M. Miller

Norman C. Miller

Mr. Charles G. Mixon and Ms. Dawn Corl

Mabel T. Miyasaki and Thomas N. Layton, PhD

Mr. Alvin Miyashiro

Mr. David M. Monsees

Mrs. Elaine Mount

Mr. Edward Munz

Bob and Beverly Murdock

Gwen Myers and Mason Myers

Katharine Myers

Mr. and Mrs. Morey M. Myers

Mr. Booker T. Nabors Jr.

Al Nettleton and Aileen Nettleton

Mr. John Neubauer and Mrs. Joan Neubauer

James and Annabel Nutter

George R. and Karen M. Offen

Catherine O'Halloran and John O'Halloran

Fredrick K. Orkin

C.H. Ozbun and Diane Ozbun

Mr. Jerrold M. Paine

Mr. Victor H. Palmieri and Mullin Consulting, Inc.

Sallie Kate Park

Mr. Herbert Parsons

Lynn D. Partin

Mr. Robert Paulen

Edward J. Pelz

John and France Pepper

Ms. Georgann S. Percival

Dr. Susan B. Perry

Harold Petersen

Virginia C. Poirier

Mr. and Mrs. Dennis Poller

Eugene S. Posnock and Christine Posnock

John and Mary Powell

Dr. Anne E. Price

Nathaniel and Mary L. Prince

Allan C. Rabinowitz

Sophie Emerson Rahman

Nancy Carol Ramsey

Dr. Brian C. Randall and Dr. Mary C. Kemen

Karen Rebb

Mr. Ronald E. Redmon and Mr. Thomas A. Normand

Mrs. Lois M. Repass

Jane Baird Resnick

Dr. Robert A. Resnik and Mrs. Mary J. Resnik

Bruce J. and Nogah Revesz

Ms. Rebecca J. Rhodes

Theresa A. Riccardi

Allyson Rice

Grace Rice

Charles A. and E. Frances Riggs

Susan F. and John Ritchie

Mr. Curtis Ritland

Robert T. Blywise Family Foundation

Mr. Jon C. Rock and Mr. Patrick Delacruz

Wavie L. Rodgers

Marie Rogers,
    In Honor of Nancy Taylor and Byron Foster

Ms. Margaret Rohdy

Herbert Rolland

Mr. Edmund J. Roman

Gordon Rosen

Ms. Clare Rosenfield

Anne Rosenzweig

Molly O. Ross

J.H. Rothwell

Dr. Jerome Rowitch

Dr. Peter Rynders and Mrs. Bernice Rynders

Jim Sadler and Kitty Ordway

Ms. Anne Sager

Dr. John Sanders

Marion W. Schafer

Joyce and Lewis Scheffey

Martin Scheinkman

Edward Schevill

M. Cathryn Schiesser and Emil R. Schiesser

Philip and Shirley Schild

Mr. John C. Schmid

Mr. Michael L. Schnell and Mrs. Rita K. Schnell

Gene Schneyer and Debra Appel

Mr. Mark W. Schwiebert

Ms. Peggy H. Scott

George and Janet Scurria

Ms. Pamela W. Sebastian

Mrs. F. Shamma

Ralph Shapiro and Shirley Shapiro

Hondo Shapley

Mr. Stephen Sharp and Mrs. Linda Jackson-Sharp

Mrs. Deanna W. Shelton

Ms. Madeline A. Shepherd

Alan M. Shiller

Lisa and Charles Siegel

Mrs. Sandra Siegmund

Helen S. Simmons

Margaret Simpson

Philip S. Slipock

Mr. James P. Snyder

Paul Vernon Snyder and Robert Britton Payne,
    In Memory of Gisela Konopka

Mary L. Spaid

Mr. John S. Spinelli

Dr. Poranee N. Sponsel and Dr. Leslie Sponsel

Milton Stapen

Ms. Robin P. Steel and Mr. Charles M. Story

Rabbi Erica Lynn Steelman

Harvey H. Stern

Ms. Ida B. Stewart and Mr. William B. Stewart

Mr. Robert Stewart,
    Robert A. Stewart Family Foundation

Sybil W. Stoller

Daniel Stone

Jerome Strobeck

Mrs. Wilma J. Struss

Mr. William Swanson

Rev. James Swartz

Bertha and Albert Swerdlow

Frank Talenfeld

Monica E. Taylor

Ms. Lou Thacker

M. Barbara W. Thomas

Dr. Virginia Cottrell Thomas

Marjorie D. Thompson

Carlisle Towery

Joänne Tromiczak-Neid

Juanita Trotter

Ms. Linda M. Umbdenstock and Mr. Fred W. Dunn

Mr. Ellor J. Van Buskirk and Mrs. Darby Van Buskirk

Warren Vietzke

P. Vigoda

Betsy Wales

Mr. Paul D. Walker

Lester D. Wallace

Virginia L. Warren

Dr. Levi Watkins Jr.

Dale Watson and Anne Watson

Sylvia B. Weaver

Mr. Joel Wellnitz

John and Laura Weymouth

Odessa Lee P. Wheeler, El-Hajj

Ms. Annette L. Wheldon

H.A. Whissen

Mr. Brad White and Ms. Barbara A. Saurer

Luwana Wiechmann-Gosch

Marianne Wilkening

Stanley Wilkosz and Michele Wilkosz

Andrea B. Williams

Mr. Robert Wing

John P. Wolff

Drs. Eric and Sandra Wolman

Ms. Sally Singleton Womer

Wanda K. Wyffels

Mr. Richard A. Zitrin,
    Arthur and Charlotte Zitrin Foundation

INDEX

PHOTO CREDITS

6   Penny Weaver

8   Michelle Leland

10   Paul Robertson

12   Courtesy of Morris Dees

15   Courtesy of Morris Dees

16   Courtesy of Joe Levin

17   Courtesy of Joe Levin

19   Joseph M. Chapman (16th Street Baptist Church);
AP Images (four little girls)

20   AP Images (marchers);
Bettmann/Corbis (troopers)

21   AP Images

22   Courtesy of the Cleveland Avenue YMCA

24   Courtesy of Morris Dees (Dees);
Paul Robertson (groundbreaking)

25   Michael Mauney

26   AP Images

27   Stanley Tretick (Dees and McGovern);
Rick Diamond (Dees and Carter)

28   Jillian Edelstein

30   James Kareles

32   AP Images

34   Courtesy of the Paradise family

35   Louis Berney

36   Courtesy of Glenda Deese

37   L. Horwitz

38   William Lovelace/Express/Getty Images

39   Rolls Press/Popperfoto/Getty Images

41   AP Images

42   Gary Settle/*The New York Times*/Redux

45   Penny Weaver

46   Christopher R. Harris

48   Penny Weaver

49   Bill Stanton

50   Courtesy of the Garner family (Garner);
Danny Welch (Garner family)

51   Penny Weaver

53   Linden Police Department

54   SPLC security

56   Sharon Steinmann

57   Courtesy of Louise Monroe

58   Dave Martin

59   Lisa Nipp

60   Matthew McVay/Corbis

62   Paul Robertson

64   John Godbey/*The Decatur Daily*

65   Bettmann/Corbis

66   D. Gorton

67   Todd Robertson

68   Courtesy of the Donald family

69   Mobile Police Department

71   © Gilles Peress/Magnum

72   Bettmann/Corbis

74   AL.com/Landov (Henry Hays);
SPLC trial exhibit (*Fiery Cross*);
AL.com/Landov (Bennie Jack Hays)

75   AL.com/Landov

76   JoAnn Chancellor

77   Lyle W. Ratliff

78   Michelle Leland

81   Randall Williams

83   Lyn Alweis/*The Denver Post*/Getty Images (Berg);
Robin Nelson/Zumapress.com (Miller)

85   Gary Nungester

86   AP Images

88   United States Marshall Service

89   Robin Nelson/Zumapress.com

90   *The News & Observer*/AP Images

91   KCTV-5/AP Images

92   Courtesy of the Seraw family

93   Brian Smale

94   Michael Lloyd/*The Oregonian*

95   Penny Weaver (Dees and Seraw);
Michael Lloyd/*The Oregonian* (Dees at trial)

96   Evan Hurd/Sygma/Corbis

98   Evan Hurd/Sygma/Corbis

99   Special to SPLC

101   Chris Kenning/*The Courier Journal*

102   MySpace (Hensley);
Meade County Sheriff (Watkins);
Joe Roy (Edwards)

103   Joe Roy (Gruver);
Brian Bohannon/AP Images (Dees)

104   Gary Stewart/AP Images

105   Jim Argo/*The Daily Oklahoman*/AP Images (Bombing);
Bob Daemmerich/AFP/Getty Images (McVeigh);
Ron Heflin/AP Images (Waco)

106   Special to SPLC

107   Courtesy of the Mansfield family (Mansfield);
Scott Houston/Sygma/Corbis

108   J. Pat Carter/AP Images

109   Special to SPLC (Kelley);
Valerie Downes (Redfeairn);
Special to SPLC (Weicherding)

110   Karen S. Doerr/*The Montgomery Advertiser* (protest);
Penny Weaver (child protestor)

111   SPLC security (child protestor);
Special to SPLC (Enemy of the People)

112   Bettmann/Corbis

113   David S. Holloway/Getty Images

114   Clarendon County Fire and Rescue
Department/AP Images

115   Keith Gedamke/*The Sumter Item*

116   Dan McComb/*The Spokesman Review*/AP Images

117   Jan Bauer/AP Images (Clinton);
Mike Groll/AP Images (Bush);
Carolyn Kaster/AP Images (Obama)

118   West Memphis Police Department/AP Images

119 David Bundy
121 Robin Henson
124 Sharon Steinmann (Baltazar-Cruz);
     Steve Liss/americanpoverty.org (booking);
     Matthew Hinton (Filipino teachers);
     Randall Williams (Wilkins);
     Sarah P. Reynolds (Julio);
     James Nachtwey (hitching post)
125 Todd Bigelow (Cooper-Harris);
     David Bundy (Frazier)
126 Courtesy of Sharron Frontiero
127 Penny Weaver (both images)
128 Special to SPLC
129 Randall Williams
131 Penny Weaver (Pugh);
     Bettmann/Corbis (Johnson);
     Owen Franken/Corbis (Wallace)
132 Tommy Giles
135 Brian Smale
136 James Nachtwey
137 James Nachtwey
139 Steve Liss/americanpoverty.org
140 Sharon Steinmann
143 Rogelio V. Solis/AP Images (both images)
144 Courtesy of the McIntosh family
145 Phoebe Ferguson
146 Dave Martin
148 Mary Beth Schultz (Brown);
     Valerie Downes (Bates)
149 Michelle Leland (Ruiz);
     Christopher Aluka Berry/alukaimages.com (Licea)
150 Special to SPLC (both images)
152 Jim McNay/*The Houston Post*
153 John Van Beekum
155 Kevork Djansezian/AP Images (Belfor);
     Valerie Downes (tree planter)

156 Brendan Hoffman/*The New York Times*/Redux
158 David Bacon
159 Lowell Handler
160 Special to SPLC
161 Special to SPLC (Nethercott);
     Special to SPLC (Leiva and Mancia)
162 Sharon Steinmann
164 Lisa Nipp
165 Dave Martin
166 Matthew Hinton
167 Armando Bellmas
169 Sarah P. Reynolds
170 Sarah P. Reynolds
171 Sarah P. Reynolds (both images)
173 Valerie Downes
174 Sam Hurd
175 Adam Taylor
176 Amy Mathers, Department of Justice (Holder);
     David Joles/*The Star Tribune*/AP Images (Rooker)
178 Jim Mone/AP Images
179 Todd Bigelow
180 Jonathan Bachman/AP Images
181 Michelle Leland (Tammy Aaberg);
     Courtesy of the Walker family (Carl Walker);
     Courtesy of the Aaberg family (Justin Aaberg)
182 Michelle Leland
184 Penny Weaver
185 Danny Welch
186 Dave Martin/AP Images (Ten Commandments);
     Penny Weaver (protest)
187 Dave Martin/AP Images (protest);
     Russell Estes (Ten Commandments removal)
188 David Bundy
189 Glenn Baeske/*The Huntsville Times* (Telleria);
     David Bundy (Oscar)
190 Thomas S. England

193 Thomas S. England
194 JoAnn Chancellor (all images)
195 Penny Weaver
196 Thomas S. England
199 Courtesy of the martyrs' families
200 Thomas S. England
202 Keith Weldon Medley
204 Alabama Tourism Department (Dees and Parks);
     JoAnn Chancellor (Memorial dedication)
205 Michelle Leland
207 Michelle Leland
208 Courtesy of Eisterhold Associates Inc. (kiosk);
     Derek Porter (theater)
209 Valerie Downes (hallway);
     Derek Porter (Wall of Tolerance)
210 Penny Weaver
212 Courtesy of Morris Dees
213 Cover illustration by Milton Glaser
214 Anthony Ellison
216 Cover illustrations by Anita Kunz, Mick Wiggins
     and David Vogin
217 Cover illustrations by Chris Buzelli, Aude Van Ryn
     and Sean McCabe
219 Jim West
220 Matthew Ludtke (two girls with stickers);
     Amy Eckert (boy holding sign);
     Joni Kabana (two girls hugging)
221 Amy Eckert (three boys);
     Allen Birnbach (two girls)
222 David Bundy
223 David Bundy
224 David Bundy (both images)
225 David Bundy (both images)
226 Michelle Leland

ACKNOWLEDGEMENTS

Like everything we do at the Southern Poverty Law Center, this book was made possible by the hard work and dedication of many people.

First and foremost, we want to thank the author, Booth Gunter, for his thorough research, keen eye for narrative and structure, and elegant prose in conveying our history as well as our vision for the future of the SPLC.

Christine Harrison was involved from the earliest stages—providing invaluable insights, research and writing.

Penny Weaver not only helped gather information and check facts but worked diligently for many years to preserve our history as editor of the *SPLC Report*. She also took many of the photographs that appear in the book.

Jamie Kizzire and Mark Potok lent their editorial skills to the project—adding polish to the final project. Michelle Bramblett and Laurie Wood helped dig up obscure information about photographs.

Everyone in the SPLC design department deserves special recognition. Michelle Leland took the lead with the initial layout and the job of matching pictures with text—a massive project that required exceptional skill and patience. Valerie Downes was there from the beginning, helping plan and organize the book when it was merely a concept. Sunny Paulk was a walking encyclopedia of knowledge when it came to SPLC pictures from the past decade. Shannon Anderson tracked down images from earlier years and did the detective work to find the photographers and secure permissions. Scott Phillips and Kristina Turner were pillars of support, contributing in numerous ways to this book and to the broader Legacy Fund project. Russell Estes provided overall art direction, adding his genius every step of the way.

All of the writing and design wouldn't have mattered without the work of Cindy Clark and Regina Jackson, both of whom worked with the printer in the planning and production stages to ensure the highest quality.

Wendy Via oversaw every stage of the planning and development while providing astute editorial guidance and perspective throughout the two-year project.

Finally, we would like to thank those outside the organization whose work informed this book—particularly Steve Fiffer, co-author of Morris' autobiography, *A Lawyer's Journey: The Morris Dees Story*. In addition, B.J. Hollars deserves special mention for his book chronicling the Michael Donald case, *Thirteen Loops: Race, Violence and the Last Lynching in America*.

—MORRIS DEES, JOE LEVIN AND RICHARD COHEN